THE GLEN EYRIE STORY
Published by Glen Eyrie
3820 North 30th St.
Colorado Springs, CO 80904
719-272-7410
www.gleneyrie.org
www.gleneyriebookstore.org

ISBN 978-0-578-92600-1

Book Design by Jasmine Morse and Patrick Kochanasz

Printed in Canada

THE GLEN EYRIE STORY

A visual history of Glen Eyrie, from General Palmer to The Navigators

The Castle
GLEN EYRIE

This book is dedicated to the
hundreds of staff members and
volunteers who have served at
Glen Eyrie from 1871 to the present.

In memory of Donald McGilchrist
and Jim Albertson

With special thanks to Len
Froisland and Betty Froisland

Left: A long-exposure night photograph of Pikes Peak and the foothills to the west of Glen Eyrie. Photograph courtesy of The Navigators Archives

CONTENTS

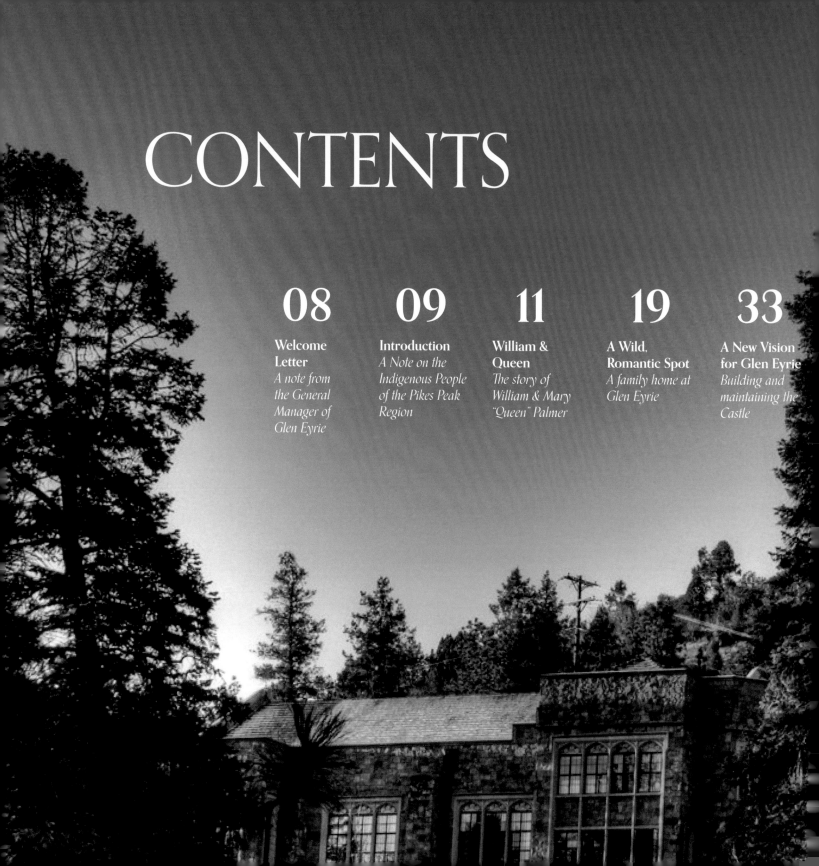

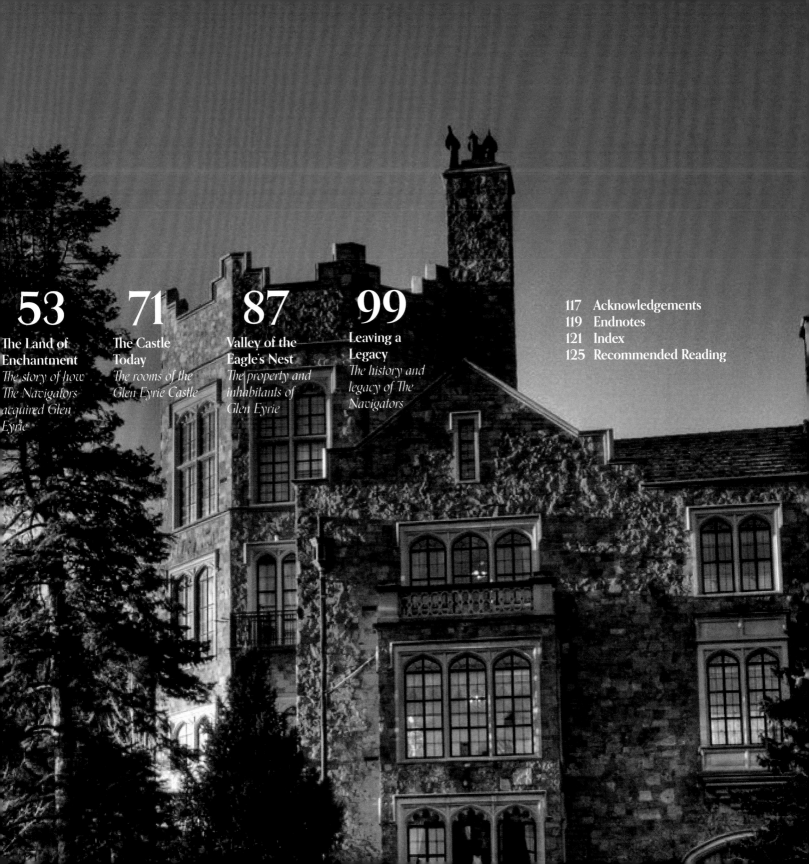

A *Letter* FROM OUR GENERAL MANAGER

Dear Friends,

I often wish that I could drive onto the property of Glen Eyrie today with General Palmer by my side. Being the hospitable and charitable man that he was, I think he would be ecstatic to see his home full of admirers, the lawns manicured and flowers abounding in the gardens at every turn! If you study the history, you will get the sense that he loved people well. Today, we hope to carry on that spirit of hospitality through the ministry of The Navigators.

For those of you have been around, you know how unique Glen Eyrie is. Just this week a friend of mine commented on how the property itself is truly a "one-of-a-kind" experience. There's nothing else like it. Former Glen Eyrie owner, George Strake, would make me chuckle when he says—"God made Glen Eyrie when He was in His best of moods." It's beautiful—absolutely! It's

hard to do justice describing its red rock spires and mammoth ponderosas to those who have never laid eyes on it. But it's more than this. The Glen is a spiritual sanctuary. People consistently tell me of how a peace came over them the moment they drove through the gates. This afternoon I met a guest in our bookstore who told me she loves to write at the back-corner table in our bookstore because it's where God speaks to her. And this evening I just got off the phone with a gentleman who told me that almost all of his major life decisions were made right here on property since he was 21 back in the 1980's. Somehow Divine access seems like it's easier to reach here.

These 723 acres are hallowed ground. They have been prayed over continually since 1953 when Dawson Trotman, the founder of The Navigators, spent 40 days up on Cedar Ridge seeking the LORD. It was there that he had a bird's eye view across the valley and down to the Castle below. Dawson inscribed his favorite Bible verses into the face of the rock. One of the passages that became particularly dear to him during this time was Deuteronomy 1:6-8 (KJV): "Ye have dwelt long enough in this mount: Turn ye, and take your journey...Behold, I have set the land before you: go in and possess the land."

Today we strive to uphold Dawson's unfolding vision of impacting people for eternity. We see Glen Eyrie as a destination retreat center. In fact our mission states: "Glen Eyrie invites our guests to focus on what really matters by creating meaningful experiences through God-honoring hospitality." We love sharing this place with others and hospitality is the vehicle through which we share our faith. We host a multitude of conferences and faith-based events, invite the public to Marriage Getaways, perform Christmas Madrigals, seasonal concerts, Castle Teas, Tours—and so many other intentionally designed experiences that draw people closer to what really matters.

As one who has the privilege of stewarding this property for the glory of God, I want to say a heartfelt "thank you" for choosing to spend time with us—we greatly appreciate your support. If by chance you have not been able to experience an overnight stay at the Glen—I invite you to get here as soon as you can! Whether life has you on the mountain top or wandering in its valleys—know that as a staff we pray that the Holy Spirit meet every person at the gate—regardless of whether or not you know the Father, and that He use this as a sacred moment in your life. Be blessed.

Grateful for you,

Dace Starkweather
Dace Starkweather
GM Glen Eyrie Castle & Conference Center

A NOTE ON THE *Indigenous People* OF THE PIKES PEAK REGION

Indigenous people were present in the Glen Eyrie region long before General William Jackson Palmer arrived on the scene in 1869. According to historian Leah Davis Witherow, "Human history in the Pikes Peak Region goes back thousands of years."[1] Stone hearths and fire rings in Garden of the Gods indicate human presence adjacent to Glen Eyrie for at least the past three thousand years. According to the Southern Ute Tribe, "There is no migration story, we were placed here in the mountains, we have always been here, we will always be here."[2] Historian Leah Davis Witherow writes, "For the Ute, this is their ancestral homeland. Culturally and historically, this is their place of being."[3]

In addition to Utes, many other tribes had ties to the region, including the Cheyenne and the Arapaho. As a cultural crossroads, the iconic red rocks at the nearby Garden of the Gods served as a landmark and meeting place. According to historian Donald McGilchrist, during the harsh winter of 1844-45 Chief Washington and the Utes used Glen Eyrie as shelter and camped there for much of the season.[4]

Right: Pikes Peak and Garden of the Gods. Photographer unknown

Right: In 1911 the El Paso County Pioneers held a celebration to commemorate the original Ute Pass Trail, and they invited the Utes back to the region for an historical exhibit and carnival. The Utes returned to the area to demonstrate their traditional way of life, in exchange for payment for their participation. Along with many of his people, Chief Buckskin Charlie returned to his birthplace near Garden of the Gods and Glen Eyrie. The event was later rebranded the "Shan Kive" and was held again in 1912 and 1913. This photograph was taken at the 1913 Shan Kive. Photograph courtesy of the Library of Congress

The establishment of Glen Eyrie as a home for the Palmer family in 1871 happened against a backdrop of complicated and often tragic relationships among the indigenous people of the region, new settlers in the area, and the United States government. These complex relationships were in place before Palmer arrived in 1869, and they continued to devolve over the following decades. The Pikes Peak Gold Rush of 1858-59 brought a wave of European Americans to the Rocky Mountains' front range. Settlers established Colorado City (initially called El Dorado) three miles south of Glen Eyrie. The town served as the territorial capital for a brief time when the new Colorado Territory was established in November 1861.

According to Witherow, "As a result of Western settlement, the indigenous people of the Pikes Peak Region were removed from a place they had been for hundreds and thousands of years."[5] In 1864, the Tabeguache Utes ceded their land east of the Continental Divide to the United States government in exchange for provisions, which the government did not supply. During the brutal winter of 1866-67, the Utes encamped at Garden of the Gods. When their resources dwindled to starvation level, they asked the residents of Colorado City for sacks of flour to survive, which they did receive. The Treaty of 1868 reduced Ute land from 56 million acres to 18 million acres and created a reservation in Western Colorado.[6]

In 1873, a group of 300-500 Utes camped at Glen Eyrie and had a peaceful encounter with General Palmer's family, who had settled in the valley in 1871. According to Chase Mellen, Palmer's young brother-in-law, "They pitched camp and pastured their ponies in a cottonwood grove along Camp Creek within the limits of Glen Eyrie and less than a mile from the house."[7] After indulging the young Mellen children's curiosity by showing them how to make arrows, the tribe members invited the Palmer family to share a meal with them.[8]

After several weeks of the encampment, former Colorado Territorial Governor Alexander Cameron Hunt asked The Utes to leave.

Tensions between indigenous people and the United States Government escalated throughout the decade. The violent Meeker Incident of 1879 resulted in the removal of the Tabeguache, and White River Utes were removed to the Uintah Reservation in Utah.

Today, although the indigenous people may have been forcibly removed from the PIkes Peak Region generations ago, they acknowledge and maintain the sacredness of this as their ancestral home. Therefore, Glen Eyrie honors the resiliency and vibrancy of the Ute, Arapaho, and Cheyenne cultures and history, because they were the first known to steward and care for the land. The Indigenous people of Colorado have living cultures and ongoing history, and they are still here today.

Chapter 1

WILLIAM *and* QUEEN

*Above: Portrait of General William Jackson Palmer, from Letters 1853-
1868/WM. J. Palmer, compiled by Isaac H. Clothier. Photograph courtesy
of The Navigators Archives*

"Do not hesitate, my darling, to tell me how much you love me,
You cannot spoil me in that way."

-William, in a letter to Queen on June 11, 1869

William Jackson Palmer was born to Matilda Jackson and John Palmer on September 17, 1836. He spent his early years at Kinsdale Farm in Delaware before the family moved to Germantown, Pennsylvania. According to historian Donald McGilchrist, "Palmer was described as somewhat stiff and reserved on the outside, but good-humored and kind in his heart. He had a remarkable persistence . . . a determination to build a neat, trim, happy and sensible world. He possessed not only persistence, but energy and vision."[9]

Bright and ambitious, William attended Boy's Central High School, a prestigious institution in Philadelphia. When he was seventeen, he went to work for the engineering department at the Hempfield Railroad and embarked on what would become his life's work.

At nineteen, his uncle Frank H. Jackson, the president of Westmoreland Coal Company, suggested that William travel to England to study the use of anthracite coal in train engines.

Young Palmer studied and traveled in England for six months, familiarizing himself with a country that would continue to play a significant role in his life. Upon returning to the United States, Palmer worked for the Westmoreland Coal Company. He then became private secretary to J. Edgar Thomson, president of the Pennsylvania Railroad.[10]

Top: Matilda Palmer, William's mother. Photograph courtesy of The Colorado Springs Pioneers Museum

Bottom: Kinsdale Farm, Delaware. Photograph courtesy of The Colorado Springs Pioneers Museum

Right: Map of the Principal Marches of the Fifteenth Pennsylvania Volunteer Calvary, from Letters 1853-1868/ WM. J. Palmer, compiled by Isaac H. Clothier. Map courtesy of The Navigators Archives

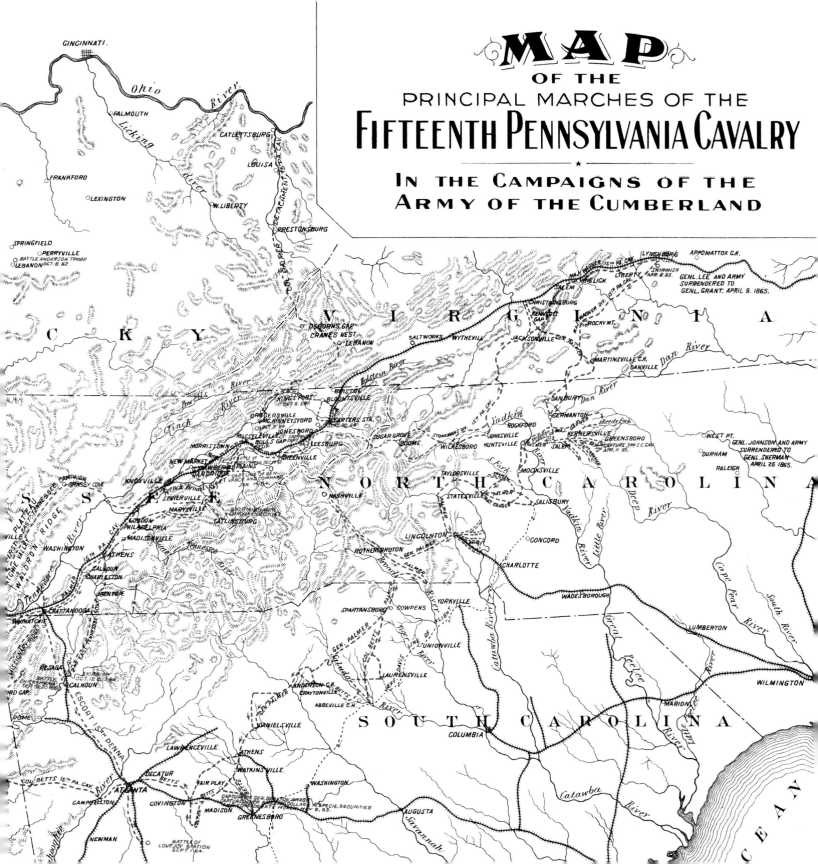

MAP
OF THE
PRINCIPAL MARCHES OF THE
FIFTEENTH PENNSYLVANIA CAVALRY
★
IN THE CAMPAIGNS OF THE
ARMY OF THE CUMBERLAND

CIVIL WAR

The Palmers were devout Hicksite Quakers. The family's religious and moral convictions led them to support abolition. In the late 1850s, William and his best friend, Isaac Clothier, organized The Young Men's Liberal Course of Lectures, a series of talks featuring luminaries of the antislavery movement, including Lucretia Mott and Wendell Phillips. [11] When the Civil War erupted in April 1861, Palmer had a difficult choice. As a Quaker, he was committed to pacifism. However, he also knew slavery was evil. In a letter to Clothier, he explained, ". . . while I believe war to be inconsistent with the teachings and example of Jesus Christ, and therefore wrong, yet I know that it would have been wrong for me to have refrained from becoming a soldier under the circumstances as they presented themselves in this country in 1861. If it be asked how I reconciled the conflicting principles, I reply that I cannot reconcile them, any more than I can reconcile the opposing mysteries of free will and fate."[12]

After deciding to join the Union Army, Palmer recruited volunteers to fight alongside him. "Palmer's object was to form a company of active, intelligent young men, of good standing in their respective communities, through the State of Pennsylvania, who would be capable of performing any military service that might be required of him."[13] In the fall of 1861, he raised an independent company called the Anderson Troop. After showing a talent for leadership with this small group, he received orders from his commanding officers to raise an entire regiment in July 1862. Palmer recruited 1,200 men to the newly organized 15th Pennsylvania Volunteer Cavalry, known as the Anderson Cavalry.

Henry McAllister was one of the best and brightest of Philadelphia who joined this effort. He was from Kent County, Delaware (Palmer's birthplace) and born three days before Palmer's own birthday. McAllister joined the troop as a private and was eventually promoted to the rank of major. The two men became lifelong friends and business associates.

Palmer had a colorful career during the war. After the Battle of Antietam, Captain Palmer crossed the Potomac into Confederate territory on an espionage mission. Enemy soldiers captured him on September 18, 1862, and he spent five tense months at prison camp Castle Thunder. To conceal his true identity as a Union captain, he concocted a fake persona, pretending to be a civilian mine inspector named W.J. Peters. He was finally released in a prisoner exchange in February 1863.[14]

Following his liberation, Palmer rejoined the 15th Pennsylvania Regiment. The men campaigned in Southeast Tennessee and Northern Georgia at the battles of Chattanooga, Lookout Mountain, and Chickamauga. During their march through the South, the regiment came across an escaped teenage slave named George Motley. Palmer liked Motley and gave him a job as a civilian orderly. The pair would remain friends the rest of their lives.

Palmer's excellence in leadership during the war attracted the attention of his commanding officers. He was awarded the Congressional Medal of Honor for leadership in battle at Red Hill, Alabama, in January 1865. Impressed with Palmer's service at Chattanooga, Major General George Thomas recommended Palmer for promotion, and in March 1865, President Abraham Lincoln confirmed Palmer for appointment to the brevet grade of brigadier general. As the Civil War entered in its final month in April, Palmer and his men chased Jefferson Davis across South Carolina and Georgia, eventually capturing his treasury wagon.

Left: William Jackson Palmer at the beginning of the Civil War in 1861. Photograph courtesy of the Colorado Springs Pioneers Museum

Above: Officers from the 15th Pennsylvania Cavalry. Back: Adjutant Josiah C. Reiff, Quartermaster John W. Johnston. Front: Major A. B. Gardner, Lieutenant Colonel Charles M. Betts, General William Jackson Palmer, Major William Wagner. Photograph courtesy of the Colorado Springs Pioneers Museum

After the war ended, Palmer returned to a career in the railroad industry. According to McGilchrist, "Palmer secured the assignment to extend the Kansas Pacific Railroad west from Kansas City. The Directors had ambitions to press on to California through New Mexico. In 1867, they requested General Palmer to survey southern routes to San Francisco from their railhead at Salina, Kansas."[15]

In the late 1860s, he located a desirable railroad route through Colorado and urged the Kansas Pacific to build there. When his employer didn't seem interested, Palmer decided to construct the route himself. From then on, he began envisioning what would become The Denver and Rio Grande Railroad.

In April 1869, Palmer met a beautiful nineteen-year-old woman named Mary "Queen" Lincoln Mellen, who was traveling with her father, William Mellen, aboard a train from St. Louis to Cincinnati. The striking beauty intrigued Palmer, and he wanted to know more about her.

Queen had been given her nickname in childhood. She was born March 26, 1850, in Prestonsburg, Kentucky. Tragedy marred her early life. In the mid-nineteenth century, infant mortality was high. Queen's two older siblings died in infancy before her birth. Her mother, Isabel, passed away from "brain fever" when the girl was four years old. Widower William Mellen then married Isabel's sister, Ellen, a common practice of the day. In addition to three surviving children from his first marriage, the new couple had seven more children and moved to Flushing, New York. Queen was a bright, tenderhearted young woman who loved art and music.

During their conversation aboard the train, Palmer fell in love with her. After their journey, the couple began a sweet courtship. They got to know one another during outings to the theater and to lectures. The pair became engaged soon thereafter.

In the midst of this romance, Palmer encountered the Pikes Peak Region for the first time. During a railroad survey in July 1869, he rode atop a carriage in the warm night air on his way to Colorado City. He awoke from a nap to find the bright moon illuminating the summit of Pikes Peak. His party camped for the night, and the next day they explored the area. They enjoyed the stunning rock formations at Garden of the Gods, the towering mountains, and the fresh summer air.

Palmer ventured into the rugged valley immediately north of the famous rock formations. To his delight, he found a magical landscape with mountains rising high to the west. A wild mixture of geological formations and life zones composed the valley. Rugged Dakota Hogback hills stood guard at the entrance to the valley. Fossilized sea creatures awaited discovery in the soft sandstone.[16] The steep canyon to the west held colorful layers of Pikes Peak Granite, Sawatch Sandstone, Peerless Dolomite, and Manitou Limestone. A sparkling stream flowed out from the canyon throughout the valley. The uplifted Lyons red rocks towered towards the bright blue sky. Although the valley was only a few short miles from the frontier settlement of Colorado City, this place seemed like it was in a world unto itself.

Palmer fell in love with the valley and determined to live the rest of his days in the scenic Colorado territory. He also dreamt of a nearby summer colony where all his friends would live. He shared his vision with Queen, telling her of his confidence that there would soon be "a famous resort"[17] near "the finest springs of soda and the most enticing scenery"[18] at the confluence of Fountain and Monument Creeks. He shared plans to build a narrow-gauge railroad running from Denver to Mexico. Palmer was excited to share this future in the Pikes Peak region with his beloved Queen.

The couple married on November 7, 1870, in Flushing, New York. They honeymooned in England, visiting friends and being tourists. Palmer also used their honeymoon trip to look for investors for the railroad, foreshadowing the competing roles that romance and business would play in his life. With investors in the United Kingdom and the United States, Palmer and his business associates, including his Civil War comrade Major Henry McAllister and Dr. William Bell, secured funding to purchase nearly 15,000 acres of land in El Paso County, Colorado.

Although it was common for railroads to create settlements along their routes to resupply the trains, Palmer wanted the colony at the base of Pikes Peak to be something special. He told Queen, "My theory for this place is that it should be made the most attractive place for homes in the west—a place for schools, colleges, literature, science, first-class newspapers and everything that the above imply."[19]

With funding in place and their recent land acquisitions, work on the railroad and the colony began in earnest. Palmer established the Denver and Rio Grande Railroad (D&RG) in 1870, the tracks of which ran from Denver southward and would eventually reach Trinidad. He formed the Colorado Springs Company to oversee the development of his proposed colony. He and his team planned one thousand acres of lots with wide streets and parks.[20] On July 31, 1871, the first stake for Fountain Colony - later renamed Colorado Springs - was driven. was driven. Town boosters promised colonists a rich cultural life, churches, bountiful sunshine, and pure mountain air. Several of Palmer's friends, including McAllister, moved to the colony to aid in its development.

With the colony and railroad underway, it was time for the Palmers to build their home in the valley they dreamed of. They established their estate in 1871, and it would serve as the family home for almost 40 years.

Chapter 2

A WILD, *romantic* SPOT

Above: Queen's Canyon. Photograph courtesy of The Navigators Archives

"What happy days we shall spend here planning and working to improve our lovely home."

-William, in a letter to Queen on July 8, 1871

A large eagle's nest on a rugged cliffside inspired the name of Glen Eyrie—Valley of the Eagle's Nest. Scottish landscape architect John Blair suggested the name after seeing the majestic birds soaring high above the valley. According to a Denver newspaper in 1871, Glen Eyrie " . . . is a wild, romantic spot, and nothing but a romantic turn of mind would have prompted any human creature to build a costly habitation in such a place. It is simply a little opening or park of a few acres, among the rocks, with a natural gateway on the east, between two great ledges of red and gray sandstone, with the mountains rising abruptly on the west, and the vast monuments and ledges of rocks on every hand worn and chiseled by time into a hundred fantastic figures."[21]

After their honeymoon, William and Queen returned to the United States. Palmer left his new bride back east while he traveled to Colorado to prepare their new home. He hired Greeley-based architect J.L. White and builder L. Whipple to design and construct a house at Glen Eyrie. Upon realizing construction wasn't going as quickly as planned, Palmer asked his father-in-law to obtain tents from the government second-hand store so that he and his new bride would have a place to live.[22] Back east, Queen was understandably less than thrilled about the prospect of moving into a tent for several months in the middle of winter. Palmer reassured her that Glen Eyrie was worth it, enticing her with the beauty of the property. He invited her to consider names for the striking rock formations. Queen chose Major Domo for the tallest rock spire, and William named the nearby canyon after her.

In October 1871, Queen arrived in the Pikes Peak region, accompanied by her father and stepmother, William and Ellen, and her young half-siblings. Palmer was away on business and unable to greet them when they arrived. How vast and rugged the Front Range of the Rockies must have seemed to Queen as she arrived in the fledgling Fountain Colony.

She and the Mellens lived in the second-hand tents in Glen

Eyrie, then moved into the upper room of the barn once that building was finished. Palmer eventually returned to the Pikes Peak Region and joined his bride. Both eagerly anticipated the completion of their house, which was delayed by harsh winter weather.

In early 1872, the home was ready at last. The family must have been relieved to move in after the lengthy construction process. The original house at Glen Eyrie was small in comparison to today's Castle, but it was luxurious for the remote Pikes Peak region in the 1870s. The original home was three and a half stories with a full basement, a gothic structure in the form of a cross. Queen had requested the unique octagonal rooms.[23] The Palmers enjoyed a parlor, dining room, library, and reception room. From the bay windows, they could enjoy the stunning canyon and rock formations. The home boasted nine fireplaces that kept everyone warm during the cold Colorado winters. In the basement were a laundry, pantry, vegetable room, and coal room. Palmer's water engineer channeled the flowing creek into an elaborate system that piped water into the house. For a house located so remotely, this was a feat of engineering.[24]

In addition to the main house and stables, Palmer had a grand vision for beautifying the entire valley. He hired landscape architect John Blair to create gardens and ponds. Blair constructed rustic wooden bridges spanning water features fed by Camp Creek. According to McGilchrist, "Within a few years, Glen Eyrie featured a willow pond where the Castle car park is now . . . a duck pond south of the Carriage House . . . a lakelet where the sports green is . . . a lily pond near Bighorn Lodge and two fish ponds near the gate. At least five arched stone bridges were thrown across Camp Creek, and these were supplemented by rustic walkways such as the one which traversed the pond between the School House and the Castle."[25] Water engineer James H. Drinkwater created an underground phreatic ditch to make the arid landscape bloom and installed beautiful fountains throughout the estate.

A glass plate image of the rocks at Glen Eyrie, unknown date. Photograph courtesy of The Navigators Archives

FAMILY LIFE

General Palmer kept a demanding travel schedule, overseeing work on the Denver and Rio Grande. In his absence, Queen spent extended periods on her own at Glen Eyrie. She enjoyed hiking around the property and loved the majestic scenery. She stayed busy by establishing the first school in Colorado Springs and organizing theatrical productions for the colonists to enjoy.

William and Queen had their first child in 1872. Queen traveled to New York for her labor, and Elsie was born on October 30. Shortly thereafter, the family returned to Colorado. Elsie loved growing up at Glen Eyrie. She

later recalled, "Of these very early days perhaps the pleasantest of all my recollections is one of [my father] and me going off alone together on a lovely summer day for a long walk. We spent hours lying in the soft grasses among the rocks of north Glen Eyrie, where the flowers were growing thick—harebells, red penstemon, kinnikinnick, and painter's brush. Our mood was a very happy one; we sang, we made up rhymes about the stealing of the hours that should have been spent in town."[26]

Along with Elsie, the Mellen children, Queen's half-siblings, lived at Glen Eyrie during those early days. In the mid-1870s, visitor Grace Greenwood reported that "children are everywhere: on the hillside, by the brookside, under the bridge, in the cañon, about the barn and all over the house."[27] There were so many exciting places to explore. When the weather was too bad to be outdoors, Elsie enjoyed playing with her toys in the Glen Eyrie playroom.

The family's fortunes changed, however. Queen's father, William, passed away, leaving his widow, Ellen, with seven children. Then the banking crisis of 1873 forced the Palmers to briefly close Glen Eyrie. They rented a small house in town, on Cascade Avenue, for several months. After their finances stabilized, they were able to return to their beloved Glen.

Above: A westward view of the house at Glen Eyrie, the Carriage House, and Queen's Canyon. Date unknown, likely late 1870s or early 1880s. Photograph courtesy of the New York Public Library

Right: Etching of Glen Eyrie, Colorado and Homes in the New West by E.P. Tenney, 1880. Courtesy of The Navigators Archives

GLEN EYRIE.

Above: John Blair designed the beautiful rustic wood bridges of Glen Eyrie. Photograph courtesy of The Navigators Archives

Middle: General Palmer in his house at Glen Eyrie with his dogs and an unknown man. Photograph courtesy of The Colorado Springs Pioneers Museum

Right: The young Palmer family at Glen Eyrie, including Elsie (atop the bridge), Queen, Dorothy, and Marjory. Photograph courtesy of The Colorado Springs Pioneers Museum

The railroad war played out in the court system and in person. In 1879, The AT&SF hired gunslinger W.B. "Bat" Masterson to seize the D&RG stations along the Front Range. Masterson recruited his friend J.H. "Doc" Holiday, and their team of sixty hired guns established a base of operations at the Santa Fe station in Pueblo. The treasurer of the D&RG decided to "borrow" the cannon at the state armory to drive out the gangsters, only to discover that Masterson had already taken the cannon himself—and had the weapon trained on the D&RG company.[29] The D&RG hired their own gunslingers, who stormed the telegraph office on the railroad platform and drove out the defenders. They then talked things over with Masterson, who surrendered.

During the railroad war and litigation process, George Gould, the son of robber baron Jay Gould, gained ownership of the D&RG and kept Palmer on as the president. Eventually, the battle reached all the way to the Supreme Court. In 1880, the court settled the dispute: The AT&SF got rights to Raton Pass, and the D&RG could build in the Royal Gorge. The victory was bittersweet, however, as Palmer had been forced out of ownership of his beloved railroad.

Dusting himself off after this challenging season, Palmer considered establishing a second railroad. With his dreams of reaching Mexico through Raton Pass dashed, he turned his full attention to the untapped potential of Southwest Colorado. His friend and business associate Dr. Bell organized a line in Utah that would eventually link up with the D&RG through the Royal Gorge.[30] In 1881, this line became known as the Denver and Rio Grande Western (D&RGW). Palmer resigned his position with the D&RG in August 1883 and turned his full attention his new D&RGW. The new narrow-gauge railroad would become a key player in the development of Southwest Colorado, linking the towns of Salida, Gunnison, Montrose, and Durango.

With the stress of the railroad war finally over, the Palmers decided to remodel their home at Glen Eyrie for the first time in 1881. They added an octagonal tower, creating an artistic sanctuary in the upper story of the tower for Queen. They also built additional barns, pools, and housing for their growing staff. The beautiful gardens at Glen Eyrie were becoming famous throughout the Pikes Peak Region. Palmer built a grapery and a conservatory that had a fountain with goldfish and lilies.[31]

The life the Palmers enjoyed at Glen Eyrie came to a precipitous end. In October 1880, Queen and her friend Alma Strettel traveled to Leadville, Colorado along the rough carriage roads. Queen was in her early 30s and eight months pregnant at the time. On their way home, Queen suffered a heart attack.[32] She survived and gave birth to her second daughter, Dorothy, shortly afterward on October 29. Unfortunately, her health continued to decline. The next year, she traveled with William to England on business and there gave birth to her third daughter, Marjory, in November 1881.

After trying to endure full-time residence at high-altitude Glen Eyrie, Queen's heart condition required a total change of elevation and scenery. In 1884, Queen and her three young daughters moved to New York, where they stayed for two years with no improvement to her health. Eventually Queen and her girls decided to settle in England without William. She had friends in the country, and the low elevation and gentle climate seemed perfect for her recovery. Although sad to be separated from her husband by an ocean, Queen was already used to spending extended seasons on her own because of Palmer's frequent travel for the D&RG. General Palmer remained in the United States, attending to his railroad business. The family stayed in touch through letters, and he visited his wife and daughters as often as he could.

Around Colorado Springs, Queen Palmer has an unfounded reputation for not being tough enough to endure life in the remote West. Historian Stephen May points out that Queen was in the unfortunate situation of simultaneously loving her husband and her new city in the Pikes Peak Region, while also craving the art, education, and other amenities of larger urban centers. She worried about her children's educational prospects on the frontier. Her health condition also increasingly necessitated the medical advice from specialists located in New York and London. According to May, "Queen . . . loved Will dearly, the record is clear, but how she was to reconcile that love with obtaining her needs became the bittersweet dilemma the rest of her life."[33]

Queen and her daughters lived in several locations throughout England. They settled into Ightham Mote in Kent in 1886. There they enjoyed the company of creative luminaries including painters Fred Jameson and John Singer Sargent. In 1890, the Palmers hired Sargent to paint Elsie's portrait, beginning the day after her seventeenth birthday. The original Sargent painting of Elsie is now at the Colorado Springs Fine Arts Center at Colorado College, and a master copy of the famous work by painter Joe Bonomo hangs in the Glen Eyrie Library. After finishing Elsie's portrait in December 1890, Sargent remained part of the Palmer women's lives. He accompanied them on excursions to the zoo and theater and included Elsie in his painting "A Game of Bowls."[34]

General Palmer expressed concern for his family's wellbeing from across the Atlantic. He and Elsie exchanged letters about why she deserved an increase in her allowance. He asked about progress on her portrait. Queen sent letters asking her husband to take a break from business life to enjoy the simple company of his small family. William traveled to England to take the family on a European tour, and they all enjoyed spending much-needed time together.

The 1893 global banking panic devastated General Palmer's investments, forcing the Palmer women to move to different accommodations in England. They first moved into Blackdown Cottage, then into Oak Cottage in Sussex.

In 1894, Queen grew weaker and weaker. She secluded herself in the upper room of the cottage so her daughters wouldn't see her terrible state. Alarmed, Elsie wired her father to come right away, and he began the long voyage across the Atlantic. He didn't arrive in time to say goodbye. Queen passed away on December 27, 1894, from pneumonia and heart failure. She was only 44 years old. Devastated over the loss of his beloved wife, General Palmer brought his daughters home to Colorado Springs. Early in 1895, the quartet settled into their new life at Glen Eyrie.

Far Left: The first renovation of Glen Eyrie in the early 1880s included expanded quarters for staff members and a tower. Photograph courtesy of The Navigators Archives

Left: Queen Palmer, 1882. Photograph courtesy of The Navigators Archives

Left top: Marjory, Dorothy, and Elsie Palmer riding horses in England. Photograph courtesy of The Colorado College Special Collections

Left bottom, left to right: Elsie Palmer, Dorothy Palmer, and Marjory Palmer. Photographs courtesy of The Colorado Springs Pioneers Museum

Right: Artist Joe Bonomo recreated John Singer Sargent's famous work 'Portrait of Miss Elsie Palmer (A Lady in White).' The original Sargent work hangs in the Colorado Springs Fine Arts Center at Colorado College. This master copy hangs in the Glen Eyrie Library. Photograph courtesy of Patrick Kochanasz

Chapter 3

A *new* VISION FOR GLEN EYRIE

Above: The scenic red rocks and beautiful trees of Glen Eyrie. Photograph courtesy of The Navigators Archives

"Such a beautiful setting required all the artistry of the architect...with the fulfillment in detail of the owner's desires and vision,"

-Edmond van Diest

The healing beauty and fresh air of Glen Eyrie was just what the grieving Palmer family needed after Queen's death. Twenty-two-year-old Elsie had spent the majority of her early childhood at Glen Eyrie, whereas fourteen-year-old Dorothy and thirteen-year-old Marjory had left when they were infants, so everything seemed new and exciting to her little sisters. General Palmer and his daughters took long hikes through Garden of the Gods and his nearby property, Blair Athol. Elsie recorded their adventures in her journals. She described an incident when Dorothy and Marjory encountered their first rattlesnake. She wrote about long afternoons on the grounds of Glen Eyrie, enjoying picnics and cooling off from the summer heat by wading in Camp Creek. On a clear evening in June 1895, the girls gazed at the stars through a telescope.[35]

In late 1902, they welcomed a holiday visit from family friend Dorothy Comyns Carr, a twenty-four-year-old artist from England.[36] On December 23, 1902, Carr looked upon the rugged, isolated Glen Eyrie landscape and remarked in her diary, "One must recreate Xmas to make it fit in this strange land!"[37] On Christmas Day, she and the Palmers opened their presents at Glen Eyrie against a backdrop of snow.

In early January 1903, the Palmers and Carr hosted the family's annual Glen Eyrie Christmas party for the children of Colorado Springs. The general sent his carriages to fetch the young guests. Palmer's staff escorted the children along the snowy Mesa to the glittering warmth of Glen Eyrie. A giant Christmas tree lit with candles and decorated with ornaments dazzled them. The kids enjoyed an evening of games, piñatas, a moving-picture show, and refreshments. There were presents too—one for each child. Palmer continued his gift-giving tradition each year. At future parties, little Dorothy Bertolotti would receive a large teddy bear, while siblings Leo and Charlotte Wolgamood received a Steiff elephant, dog, horse, and a toy stove.[38]

Left: The tower on the 1904 Glen Eyrie Castle once included a sleeping porch. After Palmer's death, the sleeping porch became infested with bees after years of disuse, so staff removed the porch. Photograph courtesy of The Navigator Archives

Middle: The original plan for the 1904 remodel of Glen Eyrie involved placing a stone veneer against the wooden siding of the house. They soon discovered that the timbers used in the home weren't strong enough to support the weight of the rock, and they tore out most of the existing structure. Photograph courtesy of The Colorado Springs Pioneers Museum

Far Right: Palmer enjoyed hosting dinner guests in his beautiful dining room. Photograph courtesy of The Colorado Springs Pioneers Museum

A NEW VISION FOR GLEN EYRIE

In 1901, General Palmer sold the Denver and Rio Grande Western Railroad. According to *The Colorado Springs Gazette* on August 15, 1901, "At the time of the sale of the Rio Grande Western about two months ago, General Palmer divided 10,000 shares of the Rio Grande dividend-paying stock 104 among all the old employees of the road. The gifts ranged in value from $2,000 to $100,000. . . . Every old employee of the road, from the section hand up, was remembered in his munificent gift."[39]

After retiring from the railroad industry, Palmer decided to transform his wooden frame house at Glen Eyrie into a beautiful stone manor. By that time, Glen Eyrie had grown significantly since its early days in the 1870s. The estate now included a cow barn, battery house, green houses and a gardener's house, a rustic lodge, and stables. With the fortune Palmer gained

during the sale of the D&RGW, it was time to turn Glen Eyrie into a place that rivaled the country homes of the wealthy industrialists of the day.

He hired construction manager Edmond van Diest, along with a team of architects and craftspeople, to make his vision a reality. Palmer brainstormed ideas for the renovations, coming up with plans that included a servant's tunnel from the Carriage House.[40] Van Diest recalled, "the rebuilding of Glen Eyrie was determined upon in 1902, although of earlier planning. The architects, Varian & Sterner, were decided upon and plans completed in the fall of 1903. During the building period the General decided upon a European tour with his three daughters, Elsie, Dorothy and Marjory, and all the work of construction of Glen Eyrie was left to me."[41]

Blueprint of the Northeast elevation of Glen Eyrie Castle. Courtesy of The Navigators Archives

·ADDITIONS·AND·ALTERATIONS·TO·'GLEN·EYRIE'·
·THE·COUNTRY·HOUSE·OF·
·GENERAL·WILLIAM·J·PALMER·

·FREDERICK·JUNIUS·STERNER·ARCHITECT·
·402·JACKSON·BLOCK·DENVER·COLORADO·

·NORTH·EAST·ELEVATION·OF·KITCHEN·WING·

·SCALE ¼ IN. TO 1 FOOT·

·NORTH·EAST·ELEVATION·
·OF·NEW·SERVANTS·QUARTERS·

Van Diest oversaw the work of regionally famous architect Frederick Sterner. For renovations to the main house, the crews intended to place a stone veneer on the wooden siding. As the masons placed the stones against the clapboard siding, it became evident that the lumber milled for the 1870s house wasn't strong enough to support the weight of the rocks. Workers tore down most of the original house. On its footprint, they created a lovely Tudor Revival manor made of moss-covered stone. According to Palmer, "while the insides of the old house were expected to remain . . . I consider the whole structure to be new."[42]

Palmer supervised the work from afar. He and his daughters went on a shopping spree in Europe, purchasing antique architectural elements for their new home. Their acquisitions surprised and frustrated van Diest. One day, General Palmer sent word that he had just bought the roof tiles off an old English manor house. Irritated, van Diest replaced the tiles he had just put on the Castle as soon as the English tiles arrived. The construction manager grew weary of his employer's last-minute changes. He later wrote, "Instructions came that odors from the kitchens must be eliminated, so a large hood over the range exhaust fan and conduit to conduct all kitchen odors about 100 feet above the house was constructed up the adjoining hillside. A bell of appropriate size must be installed on the tower with the rope accessible from within a concealed panel adjoining the dining room fireplace. Then came mantels for every room, purchased in Europe, to replace those designed by the architect and already installed. Then came the carving of the inscription over the entrance door: 'We should a guest love while he likes to stay, and when he likes not give him loving way.' A delightful thought and inscription, but not easy to execute after the stone arch had been installed."[43]

As his employees were getting frustrated with him, Palmer worried over the progress they were making. In a letter from Europe, he wondered if the tunnel could include a skylight (it could not). He also thought architect Sterner was taking too long and charging him too much money. Van Diest was called in to settle the squabble between the two men.

Despite these relational challenges, van Diest was proud of the work he and his team had done. He remarked, "There is little more than the exercise of mechanical efficiency in building the ordinary dwelling or business structure. But at Glen Eyrie there was something more. Such a beautiful setting required all the artistry of the architect, in coordination, together with the fulfillment in detail of the owner's desires and vision. Still it remained the duty of the builder to give ultimate expression to the art and skill of the architect, to remember and incorporate the countless minor details which even elaborate blueprints cannot define . . ."[44]

The stunning transformation of Glen Eyrie turned the estate into one of the most spectacular homes in the West. According to McGilchrist, "The most important undertaking by far was the complete rebuilding of Palmer's home and the extensions for the Library and Servants' Quarters, to complete what we now call the Castle."[45] A large entrance hall greeted guests when they arrived. "Concealed in the paneling were three doors leading to a lavatory, a telephone booth and an electric elevator. On the walls were heads of big game, hunting prints, and a painting of General Zebulon M. Pike."[46] A drawing room, dining room, library, and Palmer's personal den beckoned guests to explore the first floor. Beyond the dining room were the famous Glen Eyrie kitchens, a flower arranging room, butler's pantry, and a valet room.

Stepping outside the glass conservatory doors, guests would go to the recreation hall in the basement of the brand-new library wing. This space contained "a bowling alley and a billiard room. Here were sofas, bookshelves, and a Steinway piano. Nearby was a steam room lined with white tile and marble for Turkish baths."[47]

On the second story of the library wing, the grand Book Hall welcomed guests for jubilant parties. The spacious room had an imposing fireplace made of Indiana limestone, so large that workers constructed it first before building the room around it. The Book Hall was furnished with antique tables and chairs, a grandfather clock, bookshelves, and paintings.

Left: Glen Eyrie Castle. Photograph courtesy of The Navigator Archives

Right: The 1904 Glen Eyrie Castle is in the Tudor Revival style and features the style's distinctive half-timber work, overhangs, steep rooflines, focal chimneys, and natural materials. Photograph courtesy of The Navigators Archives

The new house included cutting-edge technology of the day including a central vacuum, elevator, weather register, and a fire hose that ran the three stories of the house. Nearly every bedroom had its own bathroom with indoor plumbing. Palmer's personal bathroom even had a telephone.

The home was one of the first residences in Colorado to have electricity, which Palmer generated himself at the new Electric Plant and Power House across the valley. According to van Diest, the power plant included "the boilers and coal bins, it contains the generators, motors, etc. for the heating system and the circulation pumps."[48] Electricity for the home was one thing; natural electricity created during frequent afternoon thunderstorms was another. After van Diest was nearly struck by lightning during construction, he installed a lightning rod for the property.

According to historian Dorothy Bass Spann, "Dairy and stock barns were built and a fine dairy herd imported. A Swiss dairy man and his wife, Mr. and Mrs. Louis Zehnder, were put in charge of the cattle and the dairy quarters."[49] Next to the main house, Palmer installed a pasteurization plant to purify the milk from the Glen Eyrie Dairy. In addition to the pasteurization plant, there were several other new outbuildings, including garages and barns.

The Carriage House was "capable of sheltering ten vehicles with a coach room, a saddle room, harness room."[50] The building also included "built-in bathtubs for General Palmer's dogs. He was very fond of dogs and horses and would go to great lengths for their comfort."[51] As a former cavalry officer, Palmer took great pride in his horses. For these beautiful creatures, "there was a horse stable containing 13 stalls, four box stalls, and a hospital stall."[52] He also had a dedicated team of trainers, including the talented Jesse Bass, and groomsmen who cared for the animals.

Tourists flocked to Glen Eyrie to see the stunning estate. General Palmer indulged their curiosity. According to McGilchrist, "Along this northern side of the Glen ran the Tourist Drive, to which city people were admitted to look over the Tourist Wall, drive around the fountain circle and enjoy the landscaping of Palmer's home grounds."[55] When family friend Hamlin Garland visited in the early 1900s, he remarked, "Invited to a garden party at the Glen, we entered through a most beautiful garden in which all the native shrubs and wildflowers had been assembled and planted with exquisite art . . . people were streaming in over the mountain roads . . . the General, tall, soldierly, clothed in immaculate linen and wearing a broad white Western hat, was receiving his friends . . . the garden was a wonderland of Colorado plants and flowers, skillfully disposed and scattered along the bases of the cliffs . . . the towers of the Castle were English, but the plants and blooms surrounding it were native to the Rampart hills."[56]

Left: Palmer was a devoted arborist. The landscape surrounding the Castle included a beautiful stand of trees. Photograph courtesy of The Colorado Springs Pioneers Museum

Right: The arched entrance leading into the Castle bears the inscription 'We should a guest love while he likes to stay, and when he likes not give him loving way.' Photograph courtesy of The Navigators Archives

Glen Eyrie and the Castle adjoining The Garden of the Gods Colorado Springs

"We should a guest love while he likes to stay, and when he likes not give him loving way."

-Inscription on the arched entrance leading into the Castle

Early Mazda lamps were used to illuminate Glen Eyrie's many rooms, here in the Great Hall (above detail). These lightbulbs can be seen atop one of the Great Hall's twelve-bulb chandeliers on one of the Great Hall's twelve-bulb chandeliers. Photograph courtesy of The Navigators Archives

Right: An original lightbulb found in the Castle, circa 1927. Photograph courtesy of The Navigators Archives

44

THE LIVES *of* GLEN EYRIE STAFF

The people who served on staff at Glen Eyrie are important figures. The grand country estate required a large team to prepare food, do laundry, train horses, and plant gardens. With an eye toward perfection, Palmer hired the best people he could find. From the 1870s to 1909, more than one hundred people worked at Glen Eyrie.

George Motley (1860s-1890s): Valet, assistant, courier, cook

Born into slavery in North Carolina, Motley escaped as a teenager. He came across the 15th Pennsylvania Cavalry during the Civil War. Palmer liked the young man and gave him a job as a civilian orderly. George cooked for the soldiers, and in return they taught him how to ride a horse.

Motley and Palmer had a decades-long friendship. After the war, Motley accompanied the general during his survey trips for the Kansas Pacific Railroad. George hunted game and cooked for the crew. According to historian John Holley, Motley was with Palmer in July 1869, when the pair first saw the Pikes Peak Region. Motley assisted his friend as a valet and traveling companion. He picked up mail and telegraph messages at the post office in Colorado City and delivered them to the Denver and Rio Grande office in Colorado Springs, becoming the first mail-carrier in town.

Motley married Hannah Louisa Fairbanks in 1875. He continued traveling with Palmer on D&RG business and worked at Glen Eyrie in various capacities until the late 1890s. Motley built a house in Colorado Springs and was working as a janitor in town at the time of Palmer's death in 1909. He joined Elsie, Dorothy, and Marjory at the graveside service at Evergreen Cemetery for his old friend.[53]

Charles and Amanda Robinson (1880s-1900s): Cooks

Charles Robinson fought for the Union Army in the Civil War after escaping slavery. Amanda had also escaped slavery as a young woman and met Charles in New Mexico after the war. The couple married and came to Colorado Springs in the mid-1880s. Charles joined the Glen Eyrie staff as a cook. Their daughter Mozie married Jesse Bass, General Palmer's horse trainer. The Robinsons also owned a bakery in Colorado Springs.

Bertha Williams (1889-1896, 1901-1910s): Head of laundry, cook, caretaker of the Castle

After two decades of service to the Palmer family, Williams became a caretaker at Glen Eyrie when the general died. She cooked for the remaining staff members, including Carl Fohn and the Burghard family, and oversaw operations in the main house.

Left: Male staff members at Glen Eyrie in the Carriage House, including Billy Cotzman, "Stanley Steamer", Billy Pointe, Steven Bertolotti, John Kempf, Glenn Martin, Billy Burghard, and Walter Lancashire, circa 1906. Photograph courtesy of The Navigators Archives

Right: The Bass family sitting in front of the Glen Eyrie Carriage House. Left to right: Dorothy Bass, Jesse Bass, and Mozie Bass holding baby Elsie Bass. In 'Black Pioneers of the Pikes Peak Region' by Dorothy Bass Spann

Elias "Pat" Wolgamood (early 1900s): Carpentry foreman

General Palmer was fond of the entire Wolgamood family. He gave little Leo and Charlotte a Steiff toy elephant for Christmas during one of his famous holiday parties for the town and staff children.

John C. Matthys (1898-1909): Valet

General Palmer met Matthys in England. He liked the young man and gave Matthys a temporary job as a valet during his stay in Europe. When news of the Antlers Hotel fire on October 1, 1898 reached Palmer, he made plans to leave the United Kingdom right away. He asked Matthys to come to the United States with him. When Matthys arrived in Colorado, he told Palmer he would only stay for a few months because he didn't like the arid West. However, the valet became enchanted with the Pikes Peak Region and lived at Glen Eyrie until Palmer's death.

E. Richard Brickell (1905): Stableman and stud groom

Richard and his son, Alexander, came to Glen Eyrie in 1905 to take care of The Moor and Forrest King, two of Palmer's prized horses. Richard died under mysterious circumstances in 1905. There were rumors that he was murdered by a fellow staff member after the pair got in a fight, although his death certificate indicates he probably had meningitis. Alexander was 14 when his father passed away. Palmer let the boy stay on at Glen Eyrie and made a commitment to take care of him. After the general's death, Alex worked in the tourism industry in Colorado Springs.

Florenz Ordelheide (1907-1909): Butler's assistant, caretaker for the Glen Eyrie dogs

Florenz was a newcomer to Colorado Springs in 1907, when he landed a job at the St. James Hotel. His fellow staff members advised that he could make more working for General Palmer, so he applied for a job at Glen Eyrie. Palmer hired him to assist the butler, paying him $30 a month plus room and board. Ordelheide polished the silverware and helped in the kitchens. He also fed and cared for Palmer's beloved dogs. On his days off, he enjoyed fishing in Camp Creek and taking the Great Danes on long hikes in Queen's Canyon.

Jesse Bass (early 1900s-1909): Horse trainer

Jesse Bass and his brother, Tom, were famous horse trainers in Missouri. When Palmer decided to buy Forrest King from the Bass brothers' stables, Jesse accompanied the animal to Colorado. Impressed with Bass' talents, Palmer offered him a job as his personal horse trainer. Jesse married Mozie, the daughter of Charles and Amanda Robinson. The couple lived in an apartment above the Carriage House.

Bass was one of the first people to reach General Palmer after his riding accident in 1906. He theorized that a snake or prairie dog had startled the well-trained School Boy and that the General may have been riding "loose legged," which caused the experienced rider to be thrown off the horse. After Palmer's death, Bass moved to Long Island, New York before settling in Omaha, Nebraska, where he opened his own stables.[54]

DARK DAYS

When General Palmer envisioned his future, he likely imagined the years ahead composed of family life, philanthropy, and continuing his outdoor adventures. By 1906, Elsie, Dorothy, and Marjory had grown into beautiful young women. The thriving city of Colorado Springs attracted residents and visitors from all over the world. Glen Eyrie became a center of philanthropy as Palmer donated his fortune to worthy causes. Locally, his generosity benefited the park system of Colorado Springs and tuberculosis sanitariums. Nationally, he funded the research efforts of George Washington Carver and other worthy endeavors. It seemed like Colorado and Glen Eyrie would be the center of Palmer family life forever.

Tragically, this beautiful future was not to be. On October 27, 1906, the unthinkable happened. General Palmer, his daughters, and a family friend went for a ride near Rock Ledge Ranch. William let his friend borrow his favorite horse while he rode Schoolboy, a bronco. As the party approached a gate near Glen Eyrie, Schoolboy stumbled and threw Palmer. He remained conscious after the fall but was horrified to find that he couldn't move. Doctors and neurologists rushed to Glen Eyrie to assess the situation and found that his mid-cervical spine had been injured, resulting in paralysis. As a Civil War veteran who had spent his life on horseback, the irony of this accident was not lost on General Palmer, as he later indicated to his friends.

Physician Dr. Henry Chorely Watt and a team of nurses moved into the castle to care for Palmer. After months of rehabilitation and a season of deep depression, the general turned his attention to living as fully as possible with the amount of time he had left. He bought two cars so that his chauffer, Glen Eyrie Martin (named after the Glen), could drive him around Colorado Springs. The pair explored Palmer Park, Manitou Springs, and Garden of the Gods.

With a medical team, members of the Mellen family, and his daughters all living at Glen Eyrie, things were starting to get crowded. Palmer needed peace and quiet to recover. In 1907, he decided to build the Orchard House on nearby Rock Ledge Ranch, which he had purchased from the Chambers family in 1900. His sister-in-law, Charlotte Sclater, and her new husband, William, moved out of Glen Eyrie and into the beautiful Dutch Colonial home on the ranch, giving everyone more living space.

Right: Following his riding accident in 1906 General Palmer sits in his chair with his family, including Elsie and Leopold Hamilton Myers. Photograph courtesy of The Colorado Springs Pioneers Museum

The Castle
GLEN EYRIE

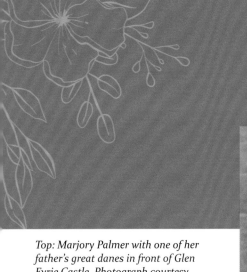

Top: Marjory Palmer with one of her father's great danes in front of Glen Eyrie Castle. Photograph courtesy of The Colorado Springs Pioneers Museum

Bottom: In 1907 the surviving members of the 15th Pennsylvania Cavalry gathered in Colorado Springs for a reunion. General Palmer and his daughters posed with the veterans on the lawn at Glen Eyrie when Palmer welcomed them to his home. Photograph courtesy of the Colorado Springs Pioneers Museum

Unable to travel for their semi-regular reunions, Palmer decided to bring the members of his old 15th Pennsylvania Volunteer Cavalry to Colorado Springs in August 1907. He paid the train fares for two hundred of his old comrades and eagerly awaited their arrival. On August 21, the Grand Army of the Republic Post of Colorado Springs greeted the soldiers in front of the Antler's Hotel. General Palmer, waiting in his car with his daughters, "passed in review receiving salutations from each comrade."[57] An afternoon thunderstorm cut short the parade.

That evening, the soldiers crowded into the Great Hall at Glen Eyrie for dinner, reliving some of their favorite wartime memories. Palmer showed them "moving pictures and recording photos,"[58] much to their delight. The next day, Major McAllister organized a trip to Cave of the Winds and a concert at Perkins Hall. That evening, veteran James Weir was excited to receive another invitation to a private dinner at Glen Eyrie, where he joined "seven of the original members of the Anderson Troop, whom I have not met for over forty years—a pleasure that seldom occurs in the voyage of life—the incident is one of many accidental rays of sunshine in our short existence here."[59]

Meanwhile, the Palmer daughters were having big adventures of their own. Marjory became engaged to Captain Wellesley, a young solider in England. In August 1907, the *Denver Rocky Mountain Daily News* reported, "It has been an open secret in the exclusive set here that if the daughters of General Palmer married it would be into the court life of England."[60]

Not to be outdone by her little sister, Elsie got engaged too. After ending a secret romantic relationship with married painter Frederick Harrison when she was younger, she remained single until her early thirties. She then decided to marry English author Leopold Hamilton Myers, who was several years her junior. Elsie and Leopold wed in a private ceremony at Glen Eyrie in January 1908. The lovely bride wore a white crepe de chine gown that had belonged to her grandmother, a beautiful gold-trimmed cape, and a crown of orange blossoms.[61]

In May of 1908, the Palmer family traveled to England for Marjory's wedding. Despite his fragile condition, General Palmer decided he wasn't going to miss it. He wired ahead to rent a steamer car in England and had his medical team carry him on a litter aboard the ship. The voyage across the Atlantic was a mixture of excitement over the impending nuptials and worry over the general's health.

To the shock of Colorado Springs residents, news of Marjory's broken engagement made headlines shortly after the wedding party had arrived in England. Rumors circulated that another woman was associated with Captain Wellesley and that perhaps he was already married. To preserve everyone's dignity, newspapers articles reported that tuberculosis patient Marjory had taken a turn for the worse in the damp climate of England. However, Marjory may have been a more active agent in her story. There's a possibility that she told her father she really wanted to marry his physician, Dr. Watt.

Regardless of the reasons behind the broken engagement, the Palmers stayed in Europe for several months as they waited for Marjory to recover from a severe downturn in her health. Perhaps the arid West was the best climate for her after all. During the voyage home in November, one of General Palmer's aides accidentally dropped him, and his head slammed against the ship's railing. Palmer survived, but the scary incident foreshadowed the end of his days.

William and Marjory returned to Glen Eyrie in late 1908. According to biographer John Fisher, "when he was back in Colorado, his strength actually seemed to revive."[62] Palmer enjoyed a visit from Elsie and his first grandchild, Elsie Queen, when the Myers family visited from England. He loved having two of his daughters home at Glen Eyrie and spent his final months surrounded by family and friends.

Left: William J. Palmer, date unknown. Photograph courtesy of The Navigators Archives

Above: William J. Palmer's signature. Courtesy of The Navigators Archives

Chapter 4

THE LAND *of* ENCHANTMENT

Above: General Palmer rides in one of his cars. Photograph courtesy of The Colorado Springs Pioneers Museum

By the spring of 1909, General Palmer's health had begun its final decline. On a snowy day in March, the general and chauffer Martin took a car ride around beautiful Glen Eyrie. It would be Palmer's last look at his beloved estate before passing away on March 13. After his death, Elsie told a friend that even in his final days, her father "was always patient, and is—I feel—the truest example of courage that I have ever known or heard of."[63]

In the years to follow, Elsie, Dorothy, and Marjory had big decisions to make about the future of Glen Eyrie. After General Palmer's will was settled, the daughters received the largest sum of Palmer's inheritors: equal portions of the estate at $713,578.13 each, paying a two percent estate tax. They wondered if they should remain at Glen Eyrie. Eventually Elsie and her husband, Leopold, decided to go back to England with their growing young family. Dorothy settled in England too, pursuing a career in social work.

In July 1909, Marjory announced her engagement to Dr. Watt, and the couple married in September. With a note of relief, *The Denver Times* reported, "the wedding of Miss Palmer culminated a series of romances that have kept society agog for the last two years."[64] After the wedding, Marjory and Dr. Watt moved into their new home at 33 West Willamette Avenue.

After the Palmer family departed, two staff families remained at Glen Eyrie. Gardeners Carl Fohn and Bill Burghard lived on the property while the Palmer daughters and their solicitor searched for a new owner. Fohn served as the superintendent of the estate and was responsible for payroll and maintaining the old Palmer standards. Burghard married his pretty fiancée, Rosa, in 1909, and the couple raised three children at Glen Eyrie. The family lived in a rustic wooden cabin below the Eagle's Nest cliff. One night a falling boulder crashed down beside their house—far too close for comfort. They moved out of their cabin and into the stone Gardener's House. In the Glen Eyrie greenhouses, Burghard continued growing his famous prize-winning chrysanthemums that General Palmer had been so fond of.

From 1909 to 1916, the Palmer daughters and their old friend Edmond van Diest tried to figure out what to do with the property. In 1910, they declined a purchase offer of $450,000 from an anonymous buyer because they weren't ready to sell. In the summers, van Diest leased the property to the Robinhood Girl's Camp and Nature Study School for use as a day camp. The campers enjoyed riding horses, doing gymnastics near the rose garden, and hiking in Queen's Canyon. In 1914, film director Romaine Fielding of the Lubin Company leased Glen Eyrie for nine months to create his masterpiece, *The Eagle's Nest*, released the following year.

Above: Marjory Palmer in her wedding dress, July 1909. Photograph courtesy of The Colorado Springs Pioneers Museum

Left: Staff members at Glen Eyrie, early 1900s. Photograph courtesy of The Navigators Archives

Right: Carl Fohn, Palmer's property manager, kept a log book of the daily activities at Glen Eyrie. The front page in this spread is the record of the day that General Palmer died on March 13, 1909. Photograph courtesy of The Navigators Archives

THE GLEN EYRIE COMPANIES

In 1914, the Palmer family decided to sell Glen Eyrie. Executor George Krause advertised the property in an auction booklet, detailing the 2,225-acre estate's charms. The booklet highlighted a grand manor house, electric lights, a power plant, dairy, reservoir system, coal house, and stables. It also featured a pasture barn, entrance lodge, cottages, a car garage, laundry, greenhouses, and swimming pools. In addition to the core valley, the Glen Eyrie property also included the old Chambers Ranch to the south of Garden of the Gods, which Palmer had purchased in 1900.

In 1916, a syndicate of investors from Oklahoma represented by Ed Dunn and Walter Eaton purchased the property. They established the Glen Eyrie Companies and intended to subdivide the valley into miniature luxury villas. An advertisement in *The Colorado Springs Gazette* from August 27, 1917, announced the sale of Glen Eyrie Villa Sites at $1,000 per site.[65]

Dunn and Eaton intended to use the existing buildings on Glen Eyrie as social centers for the new villa residents. They envisioned holding private dinners, concerts, and teas in the Great Hall. They wanted to transform rooms in the Carriage House into the Black Horse Tavern. For guests who enjoyed fishing, the company stocked the reservoirs with trout. The Glen Eyrie Company also had an ambitious plan to build a scenic road across Queen's Canyon and a tunnel through Echo Rock.

This plan was not financially viable during the First World War. An article in *The Colorado Springs Gazette* remarked that "a pretentious development project was underway by them and carried out in a large measure but the perfection of the plans were interrupted by the disturbed conditions of the war."[66] Sales of the lots didn't take off as the investors had hoped, and they were relieved when another buyer offered to take Glen Eyrie off of their hands in 1918.

RIght: In 1916 a group of investors from Oklahoma purchased Glen Eyrie with the intent to turn the property into villa sites. Brochure for the Glen Eyrie Gardens, Glen Eyrie City, and Glen Eyrie Villa Sites, approximately 1916-17. Courtesy of The Navigators Archives

ALEXANDER COCHRAN

Alexander Cochran, one of the wealthiest and most eligible bachelors in America, purchased Glen Eyrie in 1918 for $450,000. The forty-four-year-old Yale graduate had inherited $20 million from his late uncle. He managed the family business, The Alexander Smith and Son's Carpet Company, and was famous for his love of polo and yachts. An anglophile at heart, he served as a commander in the British Navy during World War I.

Unfortunately, Cochran also had tuberculosis. Upon returning to the United States following the war, he traveled throughout New Mexico and Colorado, chasing a cure. *The Colorado Springs Gazette* reported that he was frequent visitor to the Pikes Peak Region and had long admired Glen Eyrie. In addition to the existing Glen Eyrie estate, Cochran would later buy the Douglas and Lansing Ranches to the north, doubling his acreage to nearly eight thousand.

In the first year of ownership, Cochran lived in the Castle and raised cattle and pheasants on the property. He also took an active interest in the work of Carl Fohn and Bill Burghard, supporting their gardening endeavors. He also decided to build the Pink House across Camp Creek from the Castle. This new house was less costly to maintain than the Castle and located in a more cheerful spot on the sunny side of the valley. Cochran brought his love of ornithology to Glen Eyrie, exhibiting his collection of taxidermy birds in the Great Hall. He had an active social life in Colorado Springs, joining the Cooking Club, Cheyenne Mountain Club, and El Paso Club.

Two years after purchasing Glen Eyrie, Cochran entered a stormy marriage with Polish opera singer Ganna Walska. The pair met on a transatlantic voyage in 1920. The colorful Walska had been married twice before: first to a Russian count, then to her second husband, Dr. Frankel, who had recently passed away. Cochran proposed to the widow mere days after their first meeting. She initially refused, but he followed her to Paris and proposed again. Annoyed, Walska gave in and agreed to marry him.

From the start, the two didn't get along well. When Cochran proposed, Ganna was secretly in love with Harold Fowler McCormick of the International Harvester tractor family. With this romantic entanglement and Cochran's reported bad temper, divorce became imminent less than a year later. Alexander and Ganna lived separately in Paris and New York. During the divorce process, Cochran protected his real estate assets, including Glen Eyrie, by transferring them to his holding company, the Hillbright Corporation. The couple split in 1922. Ganna went on to marry three more husbands and happily spent her older years at the beautiful Lotusland estate near Santa Barbara, California, taking up yoga.

Cochran did not fare well after the divorce. He returned to Glen Eyrie only four other times. In his absence, he loaned the property to his niece, Mrs. Newbold Nages, for her honeymoon. With his health failing, he decided to sell Glen Eyrie. The Hillbright Corporation held a public auction in 1927 and advertised the property in fifty newspapers across the country.

Up for sale were two parcels of land. Parcel One was comprised of 3,591 acres, including the original Glen Eyrie property and the Chambers Ranch. Parcel Two was comprised of 3,780 acres, including the land to the north that Cochran had purchased. On August 26, 1927, Charles Stevens bid $300,000 on behalf of the Harold Lumberg Company of New York. However, neither Stevens nor Lumberg paid up, and the sale fell through. Cochran never returned to Glen Eyrie after the auction and died of pneumonia in June 1929, in Saranac Lake, New York. Tragically, the heir to Glen Eyrie, Cochran's nephew Thomas Ewing, also passed away unexpectedly.

Below: Alexander Smith Cochran, one of the wealthiest men in America, purchased Glen Eyrie in 1918. Courtesy of The Navigators Archives

Right: Cochran purchased Douglas and Lansing Ranches to the north of Glen Eyrie in the late 1910s and early 1920s, adding significance to the acreage of Glen Eyrie. Map courtesy of The Navigators Archives

COCHRAN PROPERTY

EL PASO COUNTY,

COLORADO.

Left: Alexander Cochran decided to sell Glen Eyrie at auction in 1927. Crowds packed the Great Hall and spilled out onto the lawns, curious to see who would buy the grand estate. Photograph courtesy of The Navigators Archives

Right: The 1927 auction booklet, which detailed the many beautiful features of the estate. Courtesy of The Navigators Archives

GAZETTE

SECOND NEWS AND
FEATURE SECTION

SECTION TWO

COLORADO SPRINGS, COLORADO

Purchase of Glen Eyrie Estate

PALMER SPENT $525,000 ON CASTLE ALONE

ESTATE PRACTICALLY ABANDONED SINCE BUILDER'S DEATH

Seventy years ago a great industrialist came to the then barren and unsettled Pikes peak region and selected as the most perfect site in the world for a home the Glen Eyrie territory in the Garden of the Gods. He was General William J. Palmer, Civil war hero, who became the builder of the city of Colorado

(Continued on Page Eight —Col. One)

New Owner

George Strake, Houston, Tex., oil man, who is the new owner of Glen Eyrie's 8,000 acres, five ranches, castle, canons and water system. His plans for

TELEGRAPH

FINANCIAL AUTOS
COMMUNITY ITEMS

NDAY, SEPTEMBER 25, 1938

PAGES 1 TO 8

ggest Event in Region in Years

MANY GIFTS TO PIONEERS COLLECTION

FINE CHINA FINDS WAY TO SHELVES; RARE OLD PAPERS PRESENTED

More than 2,000 persons visited the Colorado Springs Pioneer museum in August. Miss Dorothy Smith, assistant curator, who is in charge of it, found that many of the visitors wished to register and there were people from England, India, Germany and other foreign countries, as well as from almost every part of the United States. One visitor was Mrs. Lucy Barnes of Chicago, who wrote in the book that

...000
...am
was opened, and to augment the collection of the El Paso County Pi

When the Strake family purchased Glen Eyrie in 1938, it was one of the most exciting events in the area. The Colorado Springs Gazette and Telegraph proudly announced the transfer of ownership. Courtesy of The Navigators Archives

GEORGE & SUSAN STRAKE

Except for the Burghard family and their fellow caretaker, Carl Luehring, the Glen Eyrie estate sat mostly empty for nearly a decade. Finally, in 1938, George and Susan Strake of Texas purchased Glen Eyrie for $200,000. George was the owner of Strake Petroleum of Houston and had an adventurous early life, discovering the Conroe oil fields in Texas. The multimillionaire family intended to use Glen Eyrie as a summer home to escape the Houston heat and humidity.

The young Strake family enjoyed all the delights of Glen Eyrie. Their boys loved swimming in the pools and riding horses on the trails. The family also had a working ranch on the estate, including 549 cattle, thirty-three horses, two goats, and chickens. They rebuilt the water system, upgraded Eagles Nest cabin, improved the roads, and installed another swimming pool, spending $350,000 on improvements.

Devout Catholics, the Strakes were deeply honored to receive a visit at Glen Eyrie from Pope Pius XII in 1946. He decorated George Strake a Knight, Grand Cross of the Order of St. Sylvester.

In the late spring of 1947, the blissful nine years spent at their summer home came to a sudden end. A cloudburst sent a catastrophic flood down Queen's Canyon, overflowing the banks of Camp Creek and submerging much of Glen Eyrie. The flood destroyed many of the original stone bridges, washed out roads, and tore down power lines. The insurance company put the salvage price on the estate at only $100,000. Strake spent the next six years working to repair the damage, but his heart wasn't at Glen Eyrie anymore. His children had grown up and stopped spending their summer vacations with their parents in Colorado. This change in family dynamic, combined with the enormity of repair efforts, convinced Strake to sell Glen Eyrie in 1953, at a listing price of $500,000.

Left: The Strake family at Glen Eyrie. Photograph courtesy of the Strake family

Middle: Pope Pius XII visited Glen Eyrie in 1946 to decorate George Strake a Knight, Grand Cross of the Order of St. Sylvester. Photograph courtesy of the Strake family

Right: George and Susan Strake in front of Glen Eyrie Castle. Photograph courtesy of the Strake family

THE NAVIGATORS

Meanwhile, The Navigators, a California-based parachurch organization, was looking for a new home. Founded in 1933 by Dawson "Daws" Trotman as a ministry to sailors, The Navigators had outgrown their downtown Los Angeles offices. Trotman's friend Jim Rayburn, the founder of Young Life, had recently moved his organization to Colorado Springs and invited The Navigators to join him. Trotman also had a close partnership with Reverend Billy Graham, and many Navigator staff provided follow-up Bible training for Graham's famous worldwide evangelistic crusades. While The Navigators searched for a new home, Graham decided to buy a property to use as a retreat center or training academy. The two ministries entered a deal to purchase land together.

Dawson Trotman visited Colorado in 1953, searching for a suitable location. Colorado Springs real estate agent Guss Hill heard of Trotman's interest in the area through Rayburn and brought Glen Eyrie to his attention. Dawson visited the property and fell in love with its scenic beauty. He recommended the property to Graham, and the two created a plan for the Graham Association to own the estate, while The Navigators would use and maintain it. Billy and Ruth Graham visited Glen Eyrie in 1953, along with Dawson and Lila Trotman, to film promotional fund-raising movies. When the Strakes learned that two Christian ministries were interested in owning Glen Eyrie, they reduced the asking price to $300,000, plus $40,000 for furnishings.
In the end, Mr. Graham's advisors decided owning a large property would distract him from his

lifelong work of evangelistic crusades. Graham encouraged The Navigators to purchase the Glen for themselves, a major financial challenge for the small organization. There were only six weeks left on the option to buy, and the required deposit of $110,000 exceeded the ministry's annual operating budget.

Within those six weeks, The Navigators launched an ambitious fundraising appeal. Many donors gave sacrificially, selling their precious belongings, including cars and wedding dresses. The last gifts came in during the final hour on closing day in September 1953—just in time to seal the deal. In an amazing show of generosity and kindness, at the last minute, Strake included in the sale one of the old Palmer reservoirs at the top of Queen's Canyon and its surrounding land for use as a youth camp.

Since 1953, The Navigators has stewarded the legacy of this beautiful property. According to Glen Eyrie's mission statement, *"At Glen Eyrie, we promise to stay true to our Navigator legacy by purposefully and thoughtfully inspiring wonder through our hospitality, nurturing of guests, and in the natural beauty of God's creation. In this place of breathtaking grandeur, we create a uniquely sacred environment that opens the heart, mind, and soul to moments of reflection, discovery, heartening change, and genuine personal transformation, bringing our guests closer to what truly matters in life."*

Left: Dawson Trotman, Ruth Graham and Billy Graham at Glen Eyrie, 1953.
Photograph courtesy of The Navigators Archives

Top left: *George Strake and Dawson Trotman, 1953. Photograph courtesy of The Navigators Archives*

Middle: *In 1963 The Navigators held a mortgage burning ceremony to mark the 10th anniversary of the Glen Eyrie purchase. Photograph courtesy of The Navigators Archives*

Top middle: *A ticket to the dedication of Glen Eyrie in 1963. Courtesy of The Navigators Archives*

Top right: *Dawson Trotman rides a horse in the hills above the snowy Glen Eyrie valley, circa 1953-54. Dawson and his wife Lila lived in the Pink House on Glen Eyrie until Dawson's untimely death by drowning in 1956. Photograph courtesy of The Navigators Archives*

Bottom right: *Lt. James W. Downing, The Navigators' Director of Glen Eyrie, and Lila Trotman, at the Glen Eyrie dedication in 1963 on the 10th anniversary of the purchase. Photograph courtesy of the Navigators Archives*

Chapter 5

THE CASTLE TODAY

Above: Glen Eyrie Castle on a beautiful summer's day.
Photograph courtesy of Brenna Skattebo

"Enlarge the place of your tent, stretch your tent curtains wide, do not hold back; lengthen your cords, strengthen your stakes."

-Isaiah 54:2 (NIV)

The Castle at Glen Eyrie is a place of splendor—a magnificent stone fortress teeming with personal touches from the former and current occupants.

The exterior is covered with rock quarried from a local canyon. The windows and doors are carved from solid blocks of Indiana limestone, brought in by railway and carved onsite by talented craftsmen. Hooks that anchored ivy onto the walls are still embedded in the rock, and the occasional tiny fossil can be found in the limestone.

The main entrance bears a quote from The Odyssey: "We should a guest love while he likes to stay, and when he likes not, give him loving way." Such a quote exemplifies the generous, hospitable spirit of General Palmer and continues to inspire Glen Eyrie staff to strive to meet that same ideal.

Upon entering the lobby, visitors may note the ornate Italian plaster ceilings and quarter sawn oak paneled walls. The wall panels are shorter towards the ceiling, an example of forced perspective to make the ceiling seem even higher. The ornate fireplace is from fifteenth- or sixteenth-century Wales, a souvenir from the Palmers' trips across Europe. Standing guard to the left is a suit of armor from sixteenth-century Spain, affectionately known as "Carlos," a generous donation to The Navigators.

Just past the lobby is the foyer, a stunning space with glass doors at one end and a view of the front walkway at the other. This space was originally General Palmer's dining room. Nestled in one wall one are small doors through which servers passed dishes between the dining room and kitchen.

The fireplace welcomes visitors to sit, read a book, or enjoy a good conversation. Hidden behind the fireplace is one of the general's innovations—a fire hose, easily accessed by swinging open a wooden panel.

The glass doors were once part of a solarium, evidenced by the hardware attached to the ceiling to hold a second set of glass doors and by small glass panes that open like windows to let in fresh air.

Just off the foyer is the Library, which served as an after-dinner retreat for the gentlemen. There the master copy of John Singer Sargent's famous painting of the eldest Palmer daughter, Elsie, watches over the room with her unreadable expression. The painting was donated by artist Joe Bonomo, a friend of The Navigators. Sargent's original painting is housed at the Colorado Springs Fine Arts Center at Colorado College.

Legend has it that the stately fireplace in the Library tells the story of salvation with ornate wood carvings, beginning with Adam and Eve and ending with every man and woman saved by Christ. The story is played out in rich and ornate detail, carved centuries ago by monks.

Top left: The grand staircase and foyer of Glen Eyrie Castle in Alexander Cochran's era. Photograph courtesy of The Navigators Archives

Bottom left: The Castle lobby circa 2021. Photograph courtesy of Matt Anson

Middle: The ornately carved fireplace in the Castle library. Photograph courtesy of Matt Anson

Right: Detail of the historic fireplace in the Castle library. Photograph courtesy of Patrick Kochanasz

The Library leads to the Music Room, where Glen Eyrie staff serve a daily high tea surrounded by windows framing the picturesque view. The Music Room was the gathering space for ladies. It is modeled after a Louis XV salon, with ornate plaster designs adding interest to every corner and a marble fireplace enhancing the festive ambience.

Across the foyer is General Palmer's Den, boasting a large fireplace that once stretched all the way to the ceiling. During the last remodel of the Castle, architects feared Palmer's beloved fireplace was too heavy for the foundation. Because Palmer wasn't willing to lose it, they dismantled it, numbering each stone with intention to rebuild it exactly as it was. Unfortunately, due to the weight, they could only rebuild half of it.

Also on display in Palmer's Den is an annunciator box that Palmer used to summon his staff. The two original boxes were housed in the kitchen. While no longer connected to other parts of the Castle, the box is a reminder of the general's ingenuity. The names of rooms on the call box buttons were updated during Alexander Cochran's ownership in the 1920s. The Den is also home to Palmer's weathervane system. A weathervane on top of the Castle feeds information to the box in Palmer's Den, where letters glow red as the wind changes direction.

Visitors may reach the second and third floors either via the majestic staircase or by elevator. The height of innovation in General Palmer's time, maintaining the elevator today is a labor of love that requires custom replacement parts.

The next stop is the second floor. The first bedroom to the left is Palmer's room, featuring his original bed and dresser. The connected bathroom is the most ornate in the Castle, with striking blue tile, an ornate tub, and an antique telephone.

The adjacent room, accessible via a connecting door, was a sitting room. Now a parlor, the room is adorned with a chandelier and a sweeping view of the Glen Eyrie grounds and majestic rocks soaring toward the sky.

Each room includes personal touches from the Palmers' shopping spree across Europe during the last remodel of the Castle in 1904. Ornate fireplaces adorn every room, with buttons for the servant call system conveniently located next to each hearth. Stained glass transom windows crown each door, admitting light from the hallways.

Down the hall, Marjory's bedroom features a beautiful solarium. Marjory slept on this glass sleeping porch as she recovered from tuberculosis. Castle Room 206 belonged to Dr. Henry Watt, the doctor called upon to provide live-in care for the general after his accident. Dr. Watt later became Marjory's husband.

Past the family bedrooms on the second floor, a narrow hallway to the right leads to bedrooms that housed Palmer's staff members. To the left is Oriel Hall, named for the bay windows that extend from the building without reaching the ground.

The light-filled Oriel Hall leads to the Great Hall, known as the Book Hall during General Palmer's era. This magnificent room has hosted joyful gatherings from Palmer's day to the present. Here Palmer hosted his annual children's Christmas parties and the 1907 reunion of his 15th Pennsylvania Cavalry Regiment. Since The Navigators purchased Glen Eyrie in 1953, the Great Hall has been used to host Bible studies, conferences, weddings, and galas. In 1965, hundreds of young collegiate Navigator men crowded into the room for the Whing Ding conference.

Left: The Castle Foyer is the perfect place to relax in front of a cozy fire. Photograph courtesy of Matt Anson

Above: The Music Room at Glen Eyrie, set for high tea, circa 2021. Photograph courtesy of Matt Anson

Above: General Palmer and his dog sit in front of the fireplace in the den in the original Glen Eyrie house, 1870s-1880s. Photograph courtesy of The Colorado Springs Pioneers Museum

The Great Hall's limestone fireplace is the largest in the Castle. Particularly noteworthy is the method of construction. The fireplace was built first, and then the Great Hall was built around it.

A balcony overlooking the Great Hall offers a bird's-eye view of the hall below and the rocks outside the antique windows.

The third floor boasts several more bedrooms that were often used by Queen's family, the Mellens.

A narrow, winding staircase leads to the sole guest room at the top of the octagonal tower. Room 403 is the quintessential castle dream, nestled in a turret and boasting extraordinary views of the Glen Eyrie grounds.

Directly above Room 403, the Glen Eyrie bell sits atop the tower. Guests throughout the property can hear the bell ringing and echoing off the rocks during afternoon tours. In Palmer's day, the bell was used to call people in from the grounds. It was also used to alert staff to the General's riding accident in 1906. Before Colorado Springs was fully developed, the bell could be heard for miles.

Just outside the Castle, the terrace is accessible either by the glass doors from the foyer or by a winding stone staircase off Oriel Hall. With a stately fountain and magnificent view of the landscape, the terrace is a popular place for weddings, gatherings, luncheons, or just to rest and enjoy the sunshine.

Top: Palmer's room, now known as Castle 201, with the original bed, circa 2021. Photograph courtesy of Dace Starkweather

Bottom: Quen's parlor, next to Palmer's room, circa 2021. Photograph courtesy of Dace Starkweather

Above: Marjory's bedroom, circa 2021. Photograph courtesy of Dace Starkweather

Middle: Palmer's electric annunciator box was used to communicate with the Glen Eyrie staff. Photograph courtesy of Dace Starkweather

Top right: The sunroom built for Marjory, circa 2021. Photograph courtesy of Dace Starkweather

Bottom right: Marjory Palmer suffered from tuberculosis, and the sleeping porch connected to her room enabled her to get plenty of fresh air and sunshine, 1890s- early 1900s. Photograph courtesy of The Colorado Springs Pioneers Museum

Sunrise   Tower   Pinon   Gen'l   Studio
                             Palmer

Mountain   Morning

                                    Call Bell
                                    System

The Oriel Hall leads to the Great Hall.
Photograph courtesy of Matt Anson

Left: In 1907 General Palmer held a reunion of the 15th Pennsylvania Volunteer Cavalry members in the Glen Eyrie Great Hall. The soldiers ate dinner, watching a moving-picture show, and enjoyed reliving their favorite stories. Photograph courtesy of The Colorado Springs Pioneers Museum

Right, top: Today, the Great Hall hosts a variety of events including weddings, conferences, the Christmas Madrigals, and New Year's Eve balls. Photographer unknown

Right, bottom: In 1927 hundreds of people gathered inside the Glen Eyrie Great Hall to bid on the property at auction after Alexander Cochran decided to sell the estate. Photograph courtesy of The Navigators Archives

Left: The patio of Glen Eyrie Castle is a beautiful place for conference guests to have dinner on summer evenings. Photograph courtesy of Dace Starkweather

Right, top: The suite in room 301. Photograph courtesy of Dace Starkweather

Right, bottom: The tower room at Glen Eyrie. Photograph courtesy of Dace Starkweather

Chapter 6

VALLEY *of the* EAGLE'S NEST

Above: An aerial view of the Castle and grounds.
Photograph courtesy of Dace Starkweather

> *"Could one live in constant view of these grand mountains without being elevated by them into a lofty plane of thought and purpose?"*
>
> -General Palmer, in a letter to Queen

When driving through the gates at Glen Eyrie, it's easy to imagine what General Palmer saw while scouting the land that would become his home. Tall trees cast shade over a seasonal stream that flows from Queen's Canyon, a landmark the General named after his beloved wife. Stunning rocks in shades of pink and red frame the property with breathtaking views on every side. The small valley boasts more than eight miles of hiking trails offering various levels of challenge. Many trails overlook neighboring Garden of the Gods, providing a unique view of the famous landmark.

A small stone house sits next to the gate. A home for the Glen Eyrie gatekeepers in Palmer's era, it now serves as our volunteer headquarters. Dedicated volunteers tirelessly serve Glen Eyrie in every area, from tours, to construction, to maintaining the meticulously kept grounds.

The Glen Eyrie road loops past the Castle, forking off to various lodges. Just north of the intersection where the loop begins, the famed eagles' nests for which the property is named sit high on the rocks. John Blair, the general's Scottish architect, was the first to give it a name: Glen Eyrie, Valley of the Eagle's Nest. Once home to majestic golden eagles, today the nests are frequently used by red-tailed hawks.

The road also loops past the Pink House, the home Alexander Cochran built in 1925. Aptly named for the coral colored exterior, the interior of the home is beautiful and peaceful. Pink House guests enjoy cozy fireplaces and views of local wildlife on the lawn. The dining room is a miniature replica of the Glen Eyrie Great Hall, complete with oak paneling and a small balcony. The Pink House has only three guest rooms, making it one of the quietest accommodations at Glen Eyrie. Volunteer staff live at the Pink House and serve its guests.

Next to the Pink House is one of Glen Eyrie's prettiest spots, the Rose Garden. Each year, a team of volunteers carefully maintains the many different rose bushes in the garden. A tall wrought iron fence guards the flowers from wildlife looking for a snack, while shaded benches and a fountain beckon guests to stop and enjoy the beauty.

Top: The gate at Glen Eyrie in the fall. Photograph courtesy of Megan McIlvaine

Bottom: The entrance to the Pink House. Photograph courtesy of Brenna Skattebo

The rocks at Glen Eyrie are stunning in the snow.
Photograph courtesy of Dace Starkweather

Above: A vintage postcard featuring the Palmer-era Rose Garden adjacent to the Pink House, circa 1912.
Postcard courtesy of The Navigators Archives

91

Above: The current Rose Garden. Each of the roses has been planted in memorium by family members and lovingly tended by volunteer gardeners. Photograph courtesy of Dace Starkweatherurte

BIGHORN SHEEP *at* GLEN EYRIE

The state animal of Colorado, bighorn sheep are plentiful at Glen Eyrie and Garden of the Gods. The herd often grazes the Pink House lawn or surveys the land from atop the majestic rocks overlooking the Castle. The sheep can weigh more than three hundred pounds, but climb sheer surfaces with ease. In the fall, Glen Eyrie guests often hear the crack of rams' horns connecting during the rut season, the sound echoing through the valley like a rifle shot.

Colorado Parks and Wildlife maintains the health of bighorn sheep herds across the state by relocating animals from one region to another. In the 1940s, while moving eleven sheep to the western side of Pikes Peak, a Division of Wildlife truck broke down near Garden of the Gods. Having no food and inadequate housing for the animals, the driver set the sheep loose to survive on the land. This initial group of bighorn sheep became the Rampart Range herd, now one of the healthiest in North America. The same herd frequently visits Glen Eyrie today.

Glen Eyrie also hosts mule deer, wild turkeys, squirrels, migrating hummingbirds, and native bird species, as well as occasional bobcats, coyotes, bears, and mountain lions. The wild animals come and go as they please, bringing joy to guests—from a safe viewing distance!

Right: The Bighorn Sheep, often found at Glen Eyrie.
Photograph courtesy of Dace Starkweather

On the opposite side of the Pink House, Eagle's Nest Lodge was one of several cabins on General Palmer's property. It now serves as a guest lodge, where guests can sit on the front porch swings and enjoy the peaceful silence, good conversation, or resident wildlife.

Eagle's Nest sits near many hiking trails, including one that leads to a memorial site for Dawson Trotman, the founder of The Navigators. Dawson and his wife, Lila, are buried at a scenic hillside landing, high above the valley. The view from Dawson's Grave is stunning, spanning the valley and offering a picturesque glimpse of the Castle. This side of the property also features a ropes course, climbing wall, a high wire, and more.

Next to the Castle is the Carriage House that once included General Palmer's stables. It now houses the Front Desk, Glen Eyrie Bookstore and Café, and several meeting rooms aptly named after their original use: Hayloft, Granary, and Tack Room.

The Carriage House courtyard includes another of Palmer's innovations, an underground tunnel leading to the Castle. Although the Castle end is now sealed, guests can peek into the tunnel and experience a sense of mystery and wonder with the cool underground air.

Left: The entrance to the tunnel beneath the Castle. Photograph courtesy of Matt Anson

Middle: The historic Eagle's Nest Lodge. Photograph courtesy of Brenna Skattebo

Right: The Carriage House in summer. Photograph courtesy of Brenna Skattebo

The Valley of the Eagle's Nest has changed much in the past 150 years. Erosion, fires, and floods have changed the landscape significantly. Yet the same mountains that captivated Palmer still rise above the landscape. Wildlife still frequents the hilltops and grassy plains, the creek still trickles past the schoolhouse in springtime, and people still pause to wonder at the beauty of it all.

From rocky trails high above the valley to picnic tables next to the creek bed on idle summer days, Glen Eyrie offers wonder and enjoyment for visitors and staff alike. The same promise General Palmer saw during his scouting trip in 1869 still rings true today: Glen Eyrie is a natural paradise.

The hills of Glen Eyrie in the summer.
Photograph courtesy of Dace Starkweather

Chapter 7

LEAVING *a* LEGACY

*Above: The castle at Glen Eyrie. Photograph courtesy of
Brenna Skattebo*

"And the things you have heard me say in the presence of many witnesses entrust to reliable people who will also be qualified to teach others."

-2 Timothy 2:2 (NIV)

The Glen Eyrie story spans 150 years and counting. It is a story of faithfulness and God's provision. Today, Glen Eyrie is the conference and retreat ministry of The Navigators.

Nestled on more than seven hundred breathtaking acres with ninety-seven lodging rooms, Glen Eyrie's stunning beauty and rich spiritual heritage provide a place for guests to set aside their troubles and take a deep breath of fresh air. Glen Eyrie staff thoughtfully set the stage for discovery and exploration. Through group retreats, programs and conferences, historical teas and tours, or overnight stays, Glen Eyrie serves as a safe haven for transformation and inspiration.

Above: Aerial view of Glen Eyrie. Photographer unknown

The Navigators is a ministry that shares the Good News of Jesus and helps people grow in their faith through Life-to-Life® discipleship, encouraging spiritual generations of believers. Since its founding in 1933, The Navigators has upheld the mission *"To know Christ, make Him known, and help others do the same®."*

Helping others know Jesus was The Navigators founder Dawson Trotman's passion, which remains in the ministry's DNA. Dawson "Daws" Trotman was born in Arizona in 1906 and moved to Southern California as a child. After graduating high school in the mid-1920s, Dawson rebelled against his devout Christian upbringing. After several brushes with the law and a near-fatal swimming accident, Trotman decided to return to church. Hoping to impress the young ladies in his Sunday School class, he entered a Scripture memory contest. One morning in June 1926, while on his way to work, a Bible verse he had memorized flashed into his mind—John 1:12: "But as many as received him, to them gave he power to become the sons of God, even to them that believe on his name" (KJV).[67] Dawson prayed to receive Christ that day and committed to growing in his faith. He enrolled at the Bible Institute of Los Angeles and began faithfully studying the Bible, memorizing verses, praying, and telling other people about Christ.

After observing the benefits of these discipleship principles in his own life, Trotman wanted to teach them to others, echoing the call of 2 Timothy 2:2: "And the things you have heard me say in the presence of many witnesses entrust to reliable men who will also be qualified to teach others"(NIV84).[68] In 1933, Trotman extended his ministry to servicemen in the United States Navy, teaching sailor Lester Spencer the foundations of Christian growth. Gurney Harris, one of Spencer's shipmates aboard the USS West Virginia, asked about the secret of his changed life. Spencer brought Harris to Trotman, asking him to "teach Harris what you taught me." Dawson responded, "You teach him!" Spencer did teach his friend, and soon the two men were teaching others. Eventually, 125 sailors on their ship were growing in Christ and actively sharing their faith. Inspired by the similarities between sailing and navigating the Christian life, they adopted the name "The Navigators" in 1935. Their ministry emphasized prayer, Scripture memory, and sharing their faith with others.

By 1941, Navigator groups were on 50 ships in the naval fleet. Following the attack on Pearl Harbor and the United States' entry into World War II, The Navigators ministry spread to all branches of military service. Navigator homes in Seattle, Honolulu, and the Trotmans' own house in California provided places for the servicemen and women to study the Bible and gather for fun and encouragement.

In 1945, Trotman traveled around the globe to investigate the spiritual needs of the post-war world. In 1949, he sent Roy Robertson to China as the first overseas Navigator missionary. During this period, The Navigators developed a core value of helping other ministries share the Good News of Jesus. Trotman partnered with many Christian organizations, including Young Life, Wycliffe Bible Translators, and Youth for Christ. When Reverend Billy Graham asked Trotman to lead counselor training and follow-up discipleship for his Crusades, Dawson lent his own time and several of his staff members to the Graham Crusades.

Left: In 1965 hundreds of college-aged men crowded into the Great Hall for The Navigators Whing Ding. There wasn't enough space to fit everyone into the main floor and the balcony, so they built scaffolding to hold the excited crowd. Photograph courtesy of The Navigators Archives

EAGLE LAKE CAMPS

One use for the Palmer family's former home was evident as early as 1916, when The Robin Hood Girls Camp was held on the Glen Eyrie property. Nearly forty years later, George Strake gifted three hundred acres at the top of Queen's Canyon to The Navigators at the time of the Glen Eyrie purchase, with the provision that it be used as a children's camp. Dawson Trotman was delighted, as he and The Navigators already operated summer youth camps in California. With the donation of land, Eagle Lake Camps was born. Today, Eagle Lake Camps inspires Christ-centered love and commitment through counselor relationships in the midst of exciting outdoor experiences.

From its earliest days as a boys' camp, Eagle Lake became a haven for children from all over the country to get together, play hard, and have fun at one of the most unique and historic locations in America. With activities like swimming, canoeing, hiking, climbing, ziplining, and more, Eagle Lake is a kid's dream come true. Today, in addition to the main location near Woodland Park, Colorado, Eagle Lake also runs a summer day camp at Glen Eyrie and sends teams across the country to host on-location camps for churches. The dedicated staff, known as "professional kids," care for and encourage thousands of campers each summer.

Situated on a few hundred picturesque acres, Eagle Lake campers can experience the thrill of a ropes course, play on a "blob" on the lake, and connect with Christ in the beauty of His creation. Photographs courtesy of Eagle Lake

Top Right: Eagle Lake has a lasting legacy of hosting campers. Photograph courtesy of The Navigators Archives

104

The Navigators purchased Glen Eyrie in September 1953. A work crew led by John Crawford arrived at the Glen that fall. Crawford added a second story to the Electric Plant, transforming the old building into the ministry's headquarters office.

The Navigators moved their operations from Los Angeles to Colorado Springs in 1954. Many staff lived on the property, sleeping in the Castle on old second-hand Army bunks. They ate meals together in the basement of the library wing. Dawson and his wife, Lila, moved their family into the Pink House, and Daws taught Bible classes in the Great Hall for the young men and women.

Two years later, the Trotmans attended a conference at Schroon Lake, New York. On June 18, 1956, Dawson and his friends took a motorboat out onto the lake for some fun and recreation. Among the group was young Allene Beck, who could not swim. The boat hit a wave, and Dawson and Allene were thrown overboard. Dawson was able to hold the girl's head above water until she was rescued. Tragically, Dawson did not survive. He died saving the life of another at the age of 50. Billy Graham spoke at Dawson's official funeral at Glen Eyrie on June 27, 1956.

Following the death of Dawson Trotman in 1956, Lorne Sanny became president of the small ministry. The Navigators entered a period of growth, responding to promises found in Isaiah 54:2,3: "Enlarge the place of thy tent, and let them stretch forth the curtains of thine habitations: spare not, lengthen thy cords, and strengthen thy stakes; for thou shalt break forth on the right hand and on the left . . . "(KJV).[69]

Across the globe today, The Navigators is a Worldwide Partnership in which men and women who follow Christ share God's grace and love among the nations. The U.S. Navigators is just one part of a confederation of Navigator partner countries. The U.S. Navigators includes a wide variety of ministries and a broad family of missionaries, supporters, and volunteers. The ministry reaches out and mentors people in Christian faith where they work, live, worship, and play: on college campuses, military bases, in urban centers, workplaces, churches, local communities, and in hard-to-reach places.

Above, left: Musical performances were a regular part of Navigator life in the 1950s and 60s. Photograph courtesy of The Navigators Archives

Above, right: Navigator staff crowded into the dining hall at Glen Eyrie, 1960s. Photograph courtesy of The Navigators Archives

Above: College-age men and women sitting in front of the Pink House, 1960s. Photograph courtesy of The Navigators Archives

THE WALDO CANYON FIRE

"When you pass through the waters, I will be with you; and through the rivers, they shall not overwhelm you; when you walk through fire you shall not be burned, and the flame shall not consume you." -Isaiah 43:2 (NIV)

On June 23, 2012, staff members at Glen Eyrie nervously watched a column of smoke rising from Waldo Canyon to the southwest. Four miles away, at the western end of Queen's Canyon, weekend staff at Eagle Lake Camps also watched the smoke with increasing alarm. The first month of that summer was the hottest and driest June on record in Colorado. Wildfires had already destroyed thousands of acres near Fort Collins. Over the next week, the Waldo Canyon Fire would become the worst natural disaster in the history of Colorado Springs and the most costly wildfire in state history up to that time (a record that has since been surpassed). Hundreds of friends all over the world prayed for Glen Eyrie, including staff member Doug Dick, who climbed a hillside to pray just as the flames reached the edge of the property. Miraculously, Glen Eyrie was largely spared. Eagle lake lost eighty acres and a few small structures. Thermal maps of the fire's spread show "a little island" of green in the swath of the burn scar, right around Eagle Lake. Tragically, however, the fire burned 18,247 acres, destroyed 346 homes in the Mountain Shadows neighborhood, and killed two people. Nine Navigator staff members lost their homes.

In the aftermath of the fire, flash flooding became a serious concern. The Navigators embarked on an ambitious flood mitigation plan, including a large-scale reconstruction of the Camp Creek Channel and flood debris nets in Queen's Canyon. The City of Colorado Springs built a large detention pond in neighboring Garden of the Gods. During the survey work for the pond, Colorado Springs archeologist Anna Cordova discovered a large trash midden with artifacts from the Palmer days at Glen Eyrie, leading to a thrilling archaeological find.

According to Director of Operations Derek Strickler, the fire led to "a big interest in the historical significance of our property. God still has plans for this place. God is still using this place to impact people spiritually for eternity and is clearly not done with us . . . that's a humbling thing."[70]

Top: Smoke from the Waldo Canyon Fire. Photograph courtesy of Charles Jackson

Bottom Left: The Waldo Canyon Fire nearing Eagle Lake Camp. Photograph courtesy of Eddie Wright

Bottom Middle: Strike Team Leader Eddie Wright and Bill Baetge of the Targhee Wildfire Service fought the Waldo Canyon Fire at Eagle Lake Camp and protected the camp from destruction. Photograph courtesy of Susan Fletcher

Bottom Right: The aftermath of the fire near Eagle Lake Camp. Photograph courtesy of Eddie Wright

Left: Today, The Navigators help men and women know Christ through Bible Study, prayer, sharing their faith with others, and memorizing Scripture. Photograph courtesy of The Navigators

Top right: According to The Navigators U.S. President Doug Nuenke, "Having access to God, and being men and women who pray continually, means that we too can have strength of soul because of our intimate and regular fellowship with God. Our lives can be characterized by constant communication with the God of heaven and earth. And we can be like David in the Psalms, a man who celebrated the blessings of God, but also was quick to bring his concerns, gripes, and burdens to God—His stronghold and deliverer." Photograph courtesy of The Navigators

Bottom right: An illustrated Navigator pamphlet featuring Glen Eyrie, circa 1959. Courtesy of The Navigators Archives

The Navigators

CONNECTING *the* PAST *and the* PRESENT

After the devastating Waldo Canyon Fire in 2012, the City of Colorado Springs planned to install a large flood detention pond in Garden of the Gods, just north of the current property line between the park and Glen Eyrie. Whenever digging work of this nature has the potential to impact an archaeological or historic site, the project prompts a federal-level review. During the initial review process in 2013, crews conducted a shovel test at the site to check for artifacts. During the second phase of the project in 2016, Anna Cordova, lead archaeologist for the City of Colorado Springs, discovered the site held much more historical significance than anyone had first realized. Cordova "started noticing artifacts that I'd never seen before—fancy trash."[71] Upon further investigation, Cordova found bottles, pottery shards, and white enameled brick bearing the Tiffany Enameled Brick Company's mark.

Cordova consulted with Navigator historians Susan Fletcher and Donald McGilchrist to explore a possible connection with General Palmer. Fletcher and McGilchrist matched the artifacts Anna had found with objects they had in their own collection, including a Columbia dry cell battery that Palmer had used in the electric gates surrounding his property. Cordova confirmed the link to Palmer when she found an article in a 1904 issue of *The Brickbuilder Monthly* that mentioned the use of Tiffany Enameled Bricks in the construction of Glen Eyrie. From the 1870s onward, General Palmer had used the site—which had then been on his own land—to dispose of household and construction trash.

With the connection to Palmer and Glen Eyrie confirmed, a thorough study of the site was soon underway. An archaeological dig funded by FEMA and the Natural Resources Conservation Service (NRCS) commenced in the Camp Creek Valley at Garden of the Gods in the fall of 2018. The dig turned out to be the most historically significant archaeological find in the Pikes Peak Region. During the late 1800s, much household waste was thrown into public dumps, making it difficult to tell which objects belonged to specific families. This site is special because we know the items found there came from Glen Eyrie and people who lived on the property.

Staff members from Alpine Archaeology unearthed more than 65,000 artifacts, helping historians understand daily life at Glen Eyrie. According to Cordova, "Trash can tell us a lot about households and people, ethnicity, socioeconomic status, and gender. It can answer so many questions about the daily lives of these people."[72]

The artifacts bring to life stories that text-based primary resources don't tell us. For example, fancy dinnerware and the delicate bones from halibut offer a glimpse into elaborate dinner parties at the estate. Personal artifacts such as perfume bottles, a garter clip, and cosmetic jars provide insights into women's lives at Glen Eyrie. A whisk and tart pan helped to shed light on the Glen Eyrie kitchens. Many original architectural elements are present around in the Castle today. The original jigsaw puzzle tile still covers floors in the Castle's first-floor bathrooms. The terracotta roof tiles are visible on the roofline of Marjory Palmer's sunroom.

Artifacts from the Camp Creek archaeology dig are displayed at Glen Eyrie and the Colorado Springs Pioneers Museum.

Above: Anna Cordova, Lead Archaeologist for the City of Colorado Springs, examines an artifact that she found at the Camp Creek Archaeology site. Photo credit: Carol Lawrence, The Gazette. Photograph Courtesy of Anna Cordova

Right: The Camp Creek Archaeology dig unearthed over 65,000 artifacts including these bluewear dinner plates, glass bottles, and the leather upper of a shoe. Photographs courtesy of Patrick Kochanasz

112

A LEGACY OF HOSPITALITY

As the conference ministry of The Navigators, Glen Eyrie is a place of hospitality. With ninety-seven overnight rooms available on property, the Glen hosts a variety of guests, from individual travelers to large groups of conference attendees. Overnight guests can choose from three of our historic buildings or four modern lodges.

As a conference center, Glen Eyrie hosts groups large and small, including weddings, ministry conferences, business meetings, and more. Groups can enjoy dining, team building on the ropes course, private teas and tours, and other experiences tailor-made for each group's needs. They can also experience the breathtaking natural beauty of the Glen on more than eight miles of hiking trails.

Glen Eyrie is a history enthusiast's dream. Glen Eyrie Castle is listed on the National Register of Historic Places. Visitors seeking to learn more about the Palmer family, Alexander Cochran, the Strake family, and The Navigators can explore the Castle on a guided tour.

The staff at Glen Eyrie carefully stewards the historic property God provided almost seventy years ago. A large, devoted staff and volunteer team cares for the Castle and grounds. Volunteers contribute around 34,000 hours of service annually, maintaining the property, serving guests, and advancing our ministry.

One of the oldest buildings on the property, the Carriage House, was the subject of a large-scale remodel plan beginning in 2005. For this project, The Navigators received an Honorable Mention Award from the Colorado Springs Historic Preservation Alliance for Compatible Landscape design. The Carriage House is now home to the Glen Eyrie Front Desk and Palmer's Grounds Bookstore and Café. Full of ministry resources, books, gifts, and more, the Glen Eyrie Bookstore is the perfect place to enjoy a cup of coffee, a sandwich, and your next great read. NavPress, the publishing ministry of The Navigators, partners with Tyndale House Publishers, offering Bibles and books designed to inspire and draw people closer to God and each other. NavPress books are available at the Glen Eyrie Bookstore, as well as booksellers worldwide.

Glen Eyrie is many things: a historic site, a conference center, a bed-and-breakfast, a tea room, a bookstore, and more. Yet all these facets share core truths first realized in General Palmer's hospitable nature, then through the Life-to-Life® Navigator ministry approach. Glen Eyrie is a place of welcome, rest, and wonder. New and returning guests alike agree that Glen Eyrie is like no other place on earth. Full of peaceful, serene landscapes, inspiring history, and God-honoring hospitality, this unique place was set aside by God for His purposes. The Navigators and Glen Eyrie are honored to continue this legacy.

Top: The award-winning Carriage House at Glen Eyrie. Photographer unknown

Bottom left: High tea at Glen Eyrie is always an enjoyable experience. Photographer unknown

Bottom right: Palmer's Grounds Bookstore and Cafe is a great place for souvenirs, resources, and a great cup of coffee! Photograph courtesy of Dace Starkweather

GIVE A GIFT TODAY THAT HELPS THE GLEN TO THRIVE

Every Castle must have a firm foundation. At Glen Eyrie that firm foundation is YOU. As a Friend of the Glen, you are the support, the base, that helps ministry happen on this soul-stirring property. Your gift to Friends of the Glen allows our guests to experience God in intimate and personal ways.

Your gift to The Glen through being a Friend of the Glen is impacting the Kingdom in the following ways:

- Creating the perfect setting for guests to meet with God
- Providing the best possible events and spiritual retreats
- Developing the next generation of leaders
- Ensuring the most-equipped staff are a part of our team
- Stewarding our heritage and protecting our legacy for generations to come

There are two ways to give today:

1) Online: **gleneyrie.org/donate**
2) Call our Donor Care Team at **(866) 568-7827**

LEAVE A LEGACY GIFT THAT INVESTS IN TOMORROW

Since 1933, The Navigators has advanced the Gospel and built disciples for Christ. Your prayers and generosity enable us to inspire and equip generations of faithful servants. As you shape your legacy, would you consider joining many others who have planned to leave a legacy gift to The Navigators for the ministry of Glen Eyrie? By giving this way, you can model Christian stewardship to your loved ones AND extend the impact of your generosity well beyond your lifetime! We can work alongside your attorney or estate planning professional to create a charitable giving plan that supports you, your family and Glen Eyrie both today – and in the future.

Contact our Gift Planning Team

Call: **888-283-0157**
Email: **mylegacy@navigators.org**
Gift Planning Website" **mylegacy.navigators.org**

ACKNOWLEDGEMENTS

SUSAN FLETCHER

Born and raised in Colorado Springs, I am blessed to live in the ongoing dream that General William Jackson Palmer had for this beautiful city. I attended his namesake high school with a clear view of his statue in the middle of a downtown intersection. I spent my fourth year at Palmer High School writing my senior thesis about him. And I've gotten to know him better during my fourteen-year tenure as the director of history and archives for The Navigators. It's my honor to share his story with our readers and to explore all the colorful characters who have called Glen Eyrie home.

First of all, thanks to my mom and dad, Ruth and John Fletcher, for moving to Colorado Springs in the 1970s. I am grateful to have been born in the shadow of Pikes Peak. Thanks to Anton Schulzki, my high school history teacher who oversaw the thesis I wrote on Palmer, inspiring me to be a historian.

I am grateful to my colleagues at Glen Eyrie and The Navigators for their roles in preserving our history. First and foremost, my deep gratitude goes to Donald McGilchrist for taking such delight in Palmer's story and for his depth of research and writing on Glen Eyrie's history. I miss my friend very much and know he would be excited to see this book in print. Thanks to Jim Albertson for the work he did with Glen Eyrie work crews in the 1950s and 60s and for sharing the Castle's secrets with me. Thanks to the dynamic sibling duo of Len Froisland and Betty Froisland for the years they spent traveling across the state to transcribe thousands of pages of archival material about Palmer and Glen Eyrie. Their wonderful Glen Eyrie Notebooks are a treasure trove of primary source material about the property, and I am thankful for their hard work and dedication.

I am grateful to my co-author, Amy Burch, for her passion for this book and for bringing this project to life in the middle of a global pandemic. Thanks to my colleague Patrick Kochanasz for his work in preserving our archives, scanning photographs and manuscript material for the book, and his assistance and input with production design. Thanks to Jasmine Morse for her direction and execution in production design. I am thankful that each of them are on this book team.

I am thankful to my fellow historians Leah Davis Witherow, Matt Mayberry, and Dr. Katherine Sturdevant for their insightful scholarship on Palmer. I am grateful to Hillary Manion, Archivist at the Colorado Springs Pioneers Museum, for her hard work in providing Palmer-era photographs from the museum's collections for our book. I am also grateful to Delores Gustafson for her scholarship about the Mellen family. And a big thank-you to archaeologist Anna Cordova, who alerted everyone to the significance of the Camp Creek archaeology site, and to Mike Prouty and his crew from Alpine Archaeology for unearthing more than 65,000 Palmer-era artifacts.

Finally, thanks to the volunteers and staff at Glen Eyrie, who steward this beautiful historical site. I am grateful for you, and I think General Palmer would be too.

AMY BURCH

I am so grateful to God for creating and preserving such an amazing place in Glen Eyrie and allowing me to play in it.

Thank you to my parents, Terry and Betsy Burch, for always encouraging me and supporting me in every endeavor. I owe my love of reading and writing to them. They also took me on my first trips to Glen Eyrie for teas and tours and sparked a true passion in my heart for this place. I am also grateful to my brother, T.J., for believing in me always and for being ready to make me laugh at all times.

I am grateful for my friend Kelli Campbell and the entire McNamee family for nurturing my love of Glen Eyrie through high school and college. I am also grateful to Marcus Costantino for taking a chance in hiring me and mentoring me in my career, as well as for his invaluable editing advice in the project. Thank you to Kaitlin Hesch for encouraging me to join her in Glen Eyrie Guest Services. She is a dear friend and working together was a joy.

To Susan Fletcher and Patrick Kochanasz for their incredible dedication to this project, and to Jasmine Morse for her input and creativity in production design. It has been a joy to work with you and I'm beyond thrilled with what we have accomplished!

To Glen Eyrie General Manager Dace Starkweather, for his beautiful photography and for encouraging me to pursue this project, I am forever grateful.

To every person on my team, past, present, and future: you make work fun, and I am honored to work alongside you.

ENDNOTES

1. Leah Davis Witherow, "The Colorado Experience: Glen Eyrie Castle," Rocky Mountain PBS, November 2019. https://www.pbs.org/video/glen-eyrie-castle-zsgngv/ Accessed 30 March 2021.

2. "Southern Ute Tribe Chronology," Southern Ute Tribe website, https://www.southernute-nsn.gov/history/chronology/

3. Leah Davis Witherow, "The Colorado Experience: Glen Eyrie Castle," Rocky Mountain PBS, November 2019. https://www.pbs.org/video/glen-eyrie-castle-zsgngv/ Accessed 30 March 2021.

4. Donald McGilchrist, "The Gardens of Glen Eyrie," unpublished paper 2008. Navigator Archives.

5. Witherow.

6. James M. Potter, "Ute History and the Ute Mountain Ute Tribe," *Colorado Encyclopedia*, last modified April 01, 2020, https://coloradoencyclopedia.org/article/ute-history-and-the-ute-mountain-ute-tribe.

7. Chase Mellen, *Sketches of Pioneer Life and Settlement of the Great West* (New York: Unknown Binding, 1935) quoted in The Historical Garden of the Gods website, https://sites.google.com/site/thehistoricalgardenofthegods/native-american-crossroads?fbclid=IwAR0OrEy3cvabuWwXV8Ducb__7s5lSW_vNjRqaHWybzq8k535QTblzARluI8

8. Ibid.

9. Donald McGilchrist, "William Palmer Civic Vision John Jay Lecture," November 21, 2007. Unpublished paper. Navigator Archives.

10. Ibid.

11. Stephen J. May, *A Kingdom of Their Own: The Story of the Palmers of Glen Eyrie* (Colorado Springs, CO: Glen Eyrie Book Publication, 2017), 7.

12. Isaac Clothier, editor. *Letters, 1853-1868, Gen'l Wm. J. Palmer 87-88.* (Philadelphia: privately printed, 1906), 87-88.

13. Lt. Thomas Maple, "The Anderson Troop," *History of the Fifteenth Pennsylvania Volunteer Cavalry Which was Recruited and Known as The Anderson Cavalry in the Rebellion of 1861-1865*, Edited by Charles H. Kirk (Philadelphia, 1906.) 605.

14. John Fisher, *A Builder of the West: The Life of General William Jackson Palmer* (Caldwell, IO: The Caxton Printers, 1939), 90-100.

15. McGilchrist.

16. Louise Hose, "Glen Eyrie: Basic Geology," unpublished manuscript, 1990. The Navigators Archives.

17. William Palmer, letter to Queen July 1869. Quoted in Donald McGilchrist, "The Colorado Springs Colony," unpublished paper 2011. Navigator Archives.

18. Ibid.

19. William Palmer, letter to Robert Cameron, December 1871. Quoted in Donald McGilchrist, "The Colorado Springs Colony," unpublished paper 2011. Navigator Archives.

20. May, 38.

21. *The Rocky Mountain News*, October 11, 1871. Reprinted in *The Colorado Prospector*, April 1990. In The Glen Eyrie Book, Navigator Archives.

22. May, 38.

23. F.C. Thornton, "Mrs. Palmer's Splendid Part in City's Building: Striking Character of Woman," *The Colorado Springs Gazette*, April 8, 1923.

24. *The Rocky Mountain News*.

25. McGilchrist, 5.

26. John Fisher, *A Builder of the West: The Life of General William Jackson Palmer* (Caldwell, IO: The Caxton Printers, 1939), 284.

27. Grace Greenwood, quoted in "William Palmer Civic Vision John Jay Lecture," November 21, 2007. Unpublished paper. Navigator Archives.

28. Fisher.

29. Judy Suchan, "The 'War' for the Royal Gorge," *Colorado Central Magazine*, January 3, 2011.

30. McGilchrist, "History of the Glen Eyrie Gardens" Unpublished paper. Navigator Archives.

31. Fisher.

32. John Fisher, *A Builder of the West: The Life of General William Jackson Palmer* (Caldwell, IO: The Caxton Printers, 1939), 287.

33. May, 64.

34. Elsie Palmer diary, November 20, 1891, Colorado Springs Pioneers Museum, Tim Nicholson Collection, Box 5, Folder V (A):2.

35. Elsie Palmer diary, June 29, 1895, Colorado Springs Pioneers Museum, Tim Nicholson Collection, Box 5, (V) A:4.

36. Dorothy Comyns Carr diary, January 5 1903, Colorado Springs Pioneers Museum, Tim Nicholson Collection, Box 4, (V) A:5.

37. Dorothy Comyns Carr diary, December 23, 1902, Colorado Springs Pioneers Museum, Tim Nicholson Collection, Box 4, (V) A:5.

38. Dorothy Comyns Carr diary, April 27, 1903, Colorado Springs Pioneers Museum, Tim Nicholson Collection, Box 4, (V) A:5.

39. *The Colorado Springs Gazette*, August 15, 1901.

40. William Palmer, quoted in "William Palmer Civic Vision John Jay Lecture," November 21, 2007. Unpublished paper. Navigator Archives.

41. Edmond van Diest, "Building the Castle: Some Recollections By Edmond van Diest," unpublished paper, Navigator Archives.

42. William J. Palmer, letter to Edmond van Diest, December 15, 1904. Van Diest Collection, Colorado College Library. Included in The Glen Eyrie Book.

43. Van Diest.

44. Ibid.

45. McGilchrist.

46. A Trip Through Glen Eyrie with William J. Palmer," unpublished paper, Colorado College Library, Included in The Glen Eyrie Book.

47. Ibid.

48. Edmond van Diest, "Glen Eyrie Construction Costs." Unpublished manuscript. Van Diest Collection, Colorado College Library. Glen Eyrie Book.

49. Dorothy Bass Spann and Inez Hunt, "Black Pioneers of the Pikes Peak Region" (Colorado Springs, CO: Friends of the Pioneers Museum, 1990).

50. "A Trip Through Glen Eyrie."

51. "Ibid.

52. "Ibid.

53. John Holley, "Invisible People of the Pikes Peak Region," (Colorado Springs, CO: Friends of the Pioneers Museum, 1990).

54. Ibid.

55. McGilchrist.

56. Hamlin Garland, quoted in McGilchrist "History of the Gardens"

57. James Weir Diary, August 21, 1907. Colorado Springs Pioneers Museum, William Jackson Palmer Collection, Box 1.

58. Ibid

59. James Weir Diary, August 23, 1907. Colorado Springs Pioneers Museum, William Jackson Palmer Collection, Box 1.

60. "General Palmer's Daughter Engaged to English Army Officer, Hero of Boer War." *Denver Rocky Mountain Daily News*, August 25, 1907.

61. *Colorado Springs Telegraph*, January 21, 1908.

62. Fisher, 318.

63. Letter, Elsie Palmer Myers to Ida Elizabeth Weir, Colorado Springs Pioneers Museum, Elsie Queen Nicholson Collection, Box 2, Folder 2-4b.

64. "Miss Palmer Weds Physician Who Saved Life." *Denver Times*, September 14, 1909.

65. *The Colorado Springs Gazette*, August 27, 1916

66. *The Colorado Springs Gazette*, March 1, 1918.

67. John 1:12, KJV

68. 2 Timothy 2:2, KJV

69. Isaiah 54: 2-3, KJV

70. Derek Strickler, interview with Susan Fletcher October 22, 2012, Colorado Springs, CO.

71. Erinn Callahan, "Cordova Connects Springs Past and Present," *Colorado Springs Business Journal*, September 13, 2019. https://www.csbj.com/premier/profiles/youngprofessionals/cordova-connects-springs-past-and-present/article_6f397b03-9b20-5bef-9a41-65a1da877694.html

72. Anna Cordova, "The Colorado Experience: Glen Eyrie Castle," Rocky Mountain PBS, November 2019. https://www.pbs.org/video/glen-eyrie-castle-zsgngv/ Accessed 30 March 2021.

INDEX

RECOMMENDED READING

GLEN EYRIE

Anderson, George L. *General William J. Palmer; a Decade of Colorado Railroad Building*, 1870-1880. Colorado Springs, 1936.

Black, Celeste. *Queen of Glen Eyrie: The Woman Who Inspired a Castle*. Colorado Springs, CO: Glen Eyrie Book Publication, 2008.

Blevins, Tim. *Enterprise & Innovation in the Pikes Peak Region*. Colorado Springs, CO: Pikes Peak Library District with Dream City Vision 2020, 2011.

Blevins, Tim. *Legends, Labors & Loves: William Jackson Palmer, 1836-1909*. Colorado Springs, CO: Pikes Peak Library District with the Colorado Springs Pioneers Museum & Colorado College, 2009.

Fisher, John Stirling, and Chase Mellen. *A Builder of the West: The Life of General William Jackson Palmer*. Caldwell, ID: The Caxton Printers, 1939.

Fletcher, Susan. "The Palmer Daughters and Their Impact on the Colorado Springs," in *Bigwigs and Benefactors of the Pikes Peak Region*, edited by Heather Jordan, Tim Blevins, 19-42. Colorado Springs: Pikes Peak Library District, 2017.

Fletcher, Susan. "Hell and High Water: Natural Disasters at Glen Eyrie," in *Disasters of the Pikes Peak Region*, edited by Judge Dodge Cummings, 245-281. Colorado Springs, CO: Pikes Peak Library District, 2017.

Holley, John Stokes. *The Invisible People of the Pikes Peak Region: An Afro-American Chronicle*. Colorado Springs, CO: Friends of the Pioneers Museum, 1990.

Lucey, Donna. *Sargent's Women: Four Lives Behind the Canvas*. New York, NY: W.W. Norton Company, 2017.
May, Stephen J. A Kingdom of Their Own: The Story of the Palmers of Glen Eyrie. Colorado Springs, CO: Glen Eyrie, 2017.

Palmer, William Jackson, and Isaac H. Clothier. Letters, 1853-1868 / Wm. J. Palmer. Bethesda, MD: University Publications of America, 1992.

Spann, Dorothy Bass, and Inez Hunt. *Black Pioneers of the Pikes Peak Region: A History of A Pioneer Family in Colorado Springs*. Colorado Springs, CO: Little London Press, 1972.

Wilcox, Rhoda Davis. *The Man on the Iron Horse*. Manitou Springs, CO: Martin Associates, 1990.

THE NAVIGATORS

Amazing Grace, Amazing Hope: The Navigators 75th Anniversary. Colorado Springs: Navigators, 2009.

Downing, Jim. *Living Legacy: Reflections on Dawson Trotman and Lorne Sanny*. Colorado Springs, CO: DawsonMedia, 2007.

Downing, Jim. *The Other Side of Infamy: My Journey through Pearl Harbor and the World of War*. Colorado Springs: NavPress, 2016.

Fairservice, Sandy. *The Asia Legacy: Stories of Navigator Pioneers*. Singapore: Navmedia, 2007.

Fairservice, Sandy. *The Asia Legacy II: Stories of Navigator Pioneers*. Singapore: Navmedia, 2008.

Fletcher, Susan and Luke Flowers. *Extraordinary Navigators: Dawson Trotman and the Beginnings of The Navs*. Colorado Springs, CO: The Navigators History Department, 2011.

Foster, Robert D. *The Navigator*. Colorado Springs, CO: Challenge Books, 1983.

Lian, Patricia. *With Eyes Singled To His Glory: 50 Years of God's Faithfulness*. Singapore: The Navigators Singapore, 2012.

Skinner, Betty Lee. *Daws: A Man Who Trusted God: The Inspiring Life and Compelling Faith of Dawson Trotman, Founder of the Navigators*. Colorado Springs, CO: NAVPRESS, 1994.

Skinner, Betty Lee. *With Integrity of Heart and Skillful Hand: Insights from the Life and Teaching of Lorne Sanny*. Telok Kurau, Singapore.: Navigators of Singapore, 1998.

The Glen Eyrie Purchase Story. Colorado Springs, CO: Glen Eyrie, 2013.

Tift, Laverne. *Valiant in Fight: A Book of Remembrance*. Fresno, CA: Valiant Publications, 1990.

Trotman, Dawson E., Ken Albert, Susan Fletcher, and Doug Hankins. *Dawson Trotman in His Own Words*. United States: Navigators, 2014.

Wallis, Ethel. *Lengthened Cords: How Dawson Trotman Founder of The Navigators Also Helped Extend the Worldwide Reach of The Wycliffe Bible Translators*. Glendale, CA: Wycliffe Bible Translators, 1958.